A HOLY STRUGGLE

a HOLY STRUGGLE

Unspoken Thoughts of Hopkins

Margaret D. Smith
foreword by Walter Wangerin, Jr.
photography by Luci Shaw

Harold Shaw Publishers
Wheaton, Illinois

Copyright © 1992 by Margaret D. Smith

All rights reserved. No part of this book may be reproduced or transmitted in any form or by any means, electronic or mechanical, including photocopying, recording, or any information storage and retrieval system without written permission from Harold Shaw Publishers, Box 567, Wheaton, Illinois, 60189. Printed in México

ISBN 0-87788-364-5

Cover illustration is "Padre Sebastiano," by John Singer Sargent. Copyright © 1988 by The Metropolitan Museum of Art, Rogers Fund, 1910. (11.30)

Other photos copyright © 1992 by Luci Shaw

Library of Congress Cataloging-in-Publication Data

Smith, Margaret D., 1958-
    A holy struggle : unspoken thoughts of Hopkins / poems by Margaret D. Smith ; photographs by Luci Shaw.
       p.   cm. — (Wheaton literary series)
    Includes bibliographical references.
    ISBN 0-87788-364-5
    1. Hopkins, Gerard Manley, 1844-1889—Poetry.
    2. Christian poetry, American. I. Title. II. Series.
PS3569.M537638H6   1992
811'.54—dc20   91-41089
                                                                       CIP

---

99 98 97 96 95 94 93 92

10 9 8 7 6 5 4 3 2 1

TO THE POET

"I must write something, though not so much as I have to say."
HOPKINS' LETTER TO ROBERT BRIDGES, 1888

CONTENTS

*"It is in three movements,
the third returning to the first."*
LETTER TO ROBERT BRIDGES, 1884

Foreword _____ ix
Author's Preface _____ xvii

PART ONE: Sacrifice

1/ Unkempt _____ 3
2/ Plain words enough _____ 5
3/ For the novice at poor clares _____ 7
4/ This cave inside me _____ 9
5/ Which draws the world _____ 10
6/ Juice words _____ 11
7/ In certain light _____ 13
8/ Slaughter of the innocents _____ 15
9/ Pity's not an image _____ 17
10/ Leaping under stress _____ 19
11/ Kidnappers _____ 21
12/ Not willing to go _____ 23
13/ The air like wine _____ 25

PART TWO: Redemption

14/ A jar of tulips _____ 29
15/ One ventures further in _____ 30
16/ Not the place _____ 31
17/ Agony _____ 33
18/ Prometheus _____ 35
19/ Turning the earth _____ 37
20/ Raisin cakes _____ 39
21/ Settled for the black cloth _____ 41

22/	The lady's eyes	42
23/	Blue behind the veil	43
24/	The sea rain	45
25/	The mystery of Grace	47
26/	A lost one	49
27/	Bleed beauty	51
28/	Seven years	52

PART THREE: Another sacrifice

29/	Bluebell	55
30/	This pure world	57
31/	At zenith	59
32/	A wet flaming	61
33/	Clair-obscure	63
34/	Holy company	65
35/	Languishing	67
36/	No relief	69
37/	Fugue	71
38/	Revelation	73
39/	Beside me empty	75
40/	A lovely creature	76
41/	In orchards not kept	77
42/	Cloistered	79
43/	Keep Grace	81
44/	A sad and holy struggle	83

Scrapbook _____ 85
Photo Log _____ 107
Notes on the Sonnets _____ 109
Bibliography _____ 121

FOREWORD

This is a singular long poem—a sonnet sequence, in fact, a narrative that moves by patient steps, by lyric steps, by steps of an absolutely accurate observation. The poet is observing her persona, a figure modeled upon the life and character of Gerard Manley Hopkins. The persona, in a first-person, interior voice, is observing his own experience.

This is a love story.

Most of its sonnets pause, freeze time, and gaze with intensely personal eyes at the smallest of events in this minimal love. The lover himself is pausing to pay attention. And because this lover is a poet and a Jesuit, a man of liquid language, startling imagery, honesty, complexity, high spirituality, holy loyalties, and rude humanity, even small events become the *res gestae* of human experience, crucial moments in a drama of extreme importance.

On the one hand, then, this is a love story of powerful feeling and complexity. It *requires* a lyric form to find its rightest expression; it requires as well the structural restraint and capacity of an extended sonnet sequence. (Form and story are marvelously married!) Complexity: High and low the poet goes, the man who loves a nun, from joy to despair; but high and low the priest goes too, this lover of his Christ, from affairs of the flesh to affairs of the soul. His loves entwine their meanings, each illuminating the other, even as, in emotional fact, they struggle terribly together. The drama of his loving embraces, always, both the worldly and the divine (so broad and bold is Smith's endeavor here); and the conflict, or else the resolution—and certainly the persistent paradox—of the two is one of the real, remarkable, uncompromising insights of this poem into the human condition (so well does Smith accomplish her endeavor).

Within that vital tension of the loves, other tensions take their places: self-expression as both a birth and a death, a discovery and a loss of self; poetry as a sinful self-assertion, and poetry as the highest form of hymnic praise; sacramental acts as both material and spiritual, both this- and other-worldly; the character Hopkins (and, by extension, every individual) as his own particular self, with a verifiable history, and at the same time as the universal adventurer into holy territories, the observant voice of humankind. Paradox infuses this work and our world together:

> The bliss, a poem is, of being born,
> coupled with extraordinary tension,
> which is dying. One is forever torn
> from another....

On the other hand, this love story is minimal, simple, almost invisible to the soap-operatic eye. Narrative event is exceedingly spare. A novice of the Poor Clares and a Jesuit of poetical inclinations meet several times, share food, discuss his poems, share news, share (once) the confessional booth wherein their vows define them, their language is formal, restricted, and a grating separates them: she asks the blessing he renders—and then . . . nothing. The woman is cloistered. They neither meet nor speak again.

So one more significant tension is presented in the very form of this story: the least we *do,* under scrutiny of the artistic eye, in the sensitivity of a spirit self-aware, may reveal the subtle intricacy of action which we *are.* The poet at rest in a little room may be a violence after all, and the Christian, kneeling, an army at war. Saints and artists alike may be too unremarkable to be recognized by the common eye—not till they die and the interior life, perchance, is externalized.

But the very writing of the poem *is* death in the externalization:

The birth, a poem is, of death, and still
the death of it. Such longing cannot be
for long. . . .

So: a fine paradox pervades Smith's poem, the theme, the story, and the form of it. Struggle—brave tension—is its breathing spirit and its life. As a final example of paradox: its scope is broader than the lyric generally is asked to encompass these days (when poets find their particulate selves to be their most absorbing subjects), and yet the whole is accomplished in humble obedience to strict technical commandments. I honor Smith especially in this, that as she indited the terrible and faithful obedience of her Hopkins to his Christ, she manifested obedience herself even to the ancient conventions of the sonnet sequence. It is a *doing* and a *being* bound into a singular whole: she does not ask of her Hopkins what she will not attempt herself; her character is, then, what she does. The poem is performance.

* * *

In order to show the intricacy of the poem, I will twitch out one thread from the weave and make some comments about its narrative and lyric development.

I refer to the few meetings between Hopkins and "The lady from poor clares"—which meetings form a careful, dramatic progression. Images recur, deepening in meaning each time they do, deepening thereby the unspoken relationship between man and woman.

Early in the sequence, Hopkins' mute love for the woman is indicated, together with the sense of regular (devotional) encounters: they pray together (#2 and #6). But then in sonnets #7 and #8, in the midst of other renunciations ("No puddings on Sunday," and "I have no use for poems"), Hopkins renounces the lady as well:

No more to the chapel of poor clares. She
is only flesh, and flesh is death to me.

(All sorts of thematic tensions are noted therein.) But just as he *will* write poetry again, inspired by a word from her, so will he see her again—and so begins a certain grave formality in their relationship after all, each visit defined by something like ritual action.

In sonnet #13 (significantly, the last of Part One) she is mentioned for the first time since his renunciation—and they meet. She comes to him. She wakes him with a knock. Hopkins encounters "flesh." She speaks no words but brings him bread in a basket. Immediately, the bread is given a sacramental value: "I . . . swallowed a warm, white/ scrap of redemption. . . ." Perhaps this particular flesh is not death after all? Surely love receives more significance by these signs than mere heart's affection.

Part Two opens with a trip through Switzerland, Hopkins in company with his friend "Edward." Not until sonnet #20 does "the lady" reappear; but when she does, it is simply and suddenly, at her own recognizance: "The lady visited again." In place of bread—perhaps as a complication and an enrichment of that bread—she brings "raisin cakes and wine," and a book by Duns Scotus. The sacrament of her presence continues; but now her love also gives him a philosophic perceiving and peace. These seem the blessing of the lady's eyes, which eyes will fix Hopkins' attention and his imagery much hereafter, especially when they are not together: "I love the lady's violent eyes," sonnet #22. That sonnet ends with a further development of the "death" motif struck in his (now aborted) renunciation:

> In your birth,
> Lady, your eyes began to guard my breath.
> They dance between my bones and keep my death.

Sonnet #25: "I hold her eyes in mind." There is no meeting at this point, but here the two loves cross, the fleshly one and the divine one, in a breathtaking duplicity of images. Hopkins is caught and ambivalent:

> I hold her eyes in mind. Ah, no. I must
> be mindful that a woman's eyes embrace
> a poor man tighter than a snake. I trust
> the mystery of Grace will not erase
> my memory of holy love but bind
> me to my dearest Heart, or I be blind.

Well, the fascinating badness of the snake may be an obvious ambiguity; not so obvious yet is the "mystery of Grace," which is both the core of Christian doctrine and the name of the lady of Poor Clares. So which *is* the "holy love," and which *is* his "dearest Heart" after all?

We are well prepared for the next formal meeting, sonnet #27, when the lady again brings something to the poet. This "something" must be as sacramental as bread and wine, as much a way of seeing as Duns Scotus and the "eyes" of the lady that "guard my breath." What does she bring? News. And the catalyst of poetry again:

> Again across the field she visited,
> this time with eyes like pewter suns
> and news of death.

"Death" takes deeper and deeper meaning. Here, five Franciscan nuns drowned when *The Deutschland* wrecked. But poetry is a dying, too, and poetry stirs in Hopkins' heart like bloody death:

> If I began to spill my heart's red song,
> I would not stop—my heart's pang, shiver,
> long fire, I could not stop—my heart's blood river...

Here is a marvelous height of impassioned language, exactly when Hopkins calls upon language again. And the dramatic expression is exactly right: a sentence without ending, spilling into poetry hereafter.

It is not accidental that the next sonnet is the last in Part Two, since in it all these established images are brought together: the name of the lady is finally revealed, the sacramental element of her presence clearly acknowledged, the grave ambiguity of his several lovings underscored, the bloody mix of poetry and death, the tension between poetic expression and personal, intimate silence, for here he indites in a poem the love he never, never speaks to the lady, Grace:

> Lady, Grace, what is not spoken of—
> though wildly sung through veins from the heart's rim—
> is blood of the beloved, holy love.
> What have we spoken, these seven slim
> years, to one another? A silent vow,
> as when bodies pass the Body, we took
> at first blush. Except for greetings now
> and again, we seem as quiet as a book.
> But when you came to me, piercing your heart
> for your sisters, what bright language your body
> spilled! These seven years I have lived apart,
> to kill the passions. But now may God
> be with us as we speak. May grace be bread
> for us. And may our love be still unsaid.

Can one fail here to suffer ambiguity of the flesh, the host, the Body of Christ, the mortal bodies of human beings, the blood of the Crucified—or the blood of the sacrifice of fleshly silence, the pain of never touching one's beloved, except as two touch the same bread they eat in the sacrament?

The breadth and the passion and the complexity of this sonnet derives from the sonnets that precede it. Each ritual visit, complete in itself, bears meaning toward this, the spiritual encounter that is the clear ("unsaid") declaration of love within the poet/priest Hopkins for grace/Grace.

In a dream, in sonnet #32, one more ritual meeting so like the others—one more before their final confessional meeting (and his benediction)—ends all meetings forever. That it is only a dream, and that it is so like their earlier spontaneous and innocent meetings, causes pathos:

> The morning fair and cloudless, Grace
> appeared with biscuits, a kindness.

* * *

Light and quick as this reading is, I mean only to say: Pay attention! *A Holy Struggle* deserves attention, both common and critical. This bountiful poem will last, yielding better and better things to scrutinies wiser and more incisive than mine.

Walter Wangerin, Jr.
March 4, 1991

AUTHOR'S PREFACE

Reading Hopkins' letters, journals and notes
one could easily believe that he
could *think* in sonnet form. His anecdotes
on bluebells contain, like his poetry,
original, chiseled phrases blasted
open by the energy of root forms.
Hopkins would be shocked by what has lasted
a century: jottings on lightning storms;
a quick note to Coventry Patmore. What
Hopkins *never* wrote, however, he may
have thought too dangerous for words: his gut
and heart reaction to a woman's grey
eyes, for instance. I thought to write this book
on thoughts he could not speak. In sonnets: look.

To be honest I'll admit, though this time not in sonnet form, that Hopkins' own writings weave through and through these poems. Nearly all of the epigraphs, as well as many of the sonnets' germinations, come from a hand-sized collection of his selected work printed in 1960 by Penguin Books as *Poems and Prose of Gerard Manley Hopkins,* W. H. Gardner, editor.

But this book of sonnets is not meant to be an historical biography of Hopkins. The best account of his life must be Eleanor

Ruggles' *Gerard Manley Hopkins: A Life*. Ruggles' book is so painstakingly researched that when Luci Shaw and I tramped around England, Wales, and Ireland to visit Hopkins' old haunts, we used *GMH: A Life* as a guidebook. My book is not a biography but a simple fiction based on Hopkins' adult writing years, which thinly spanned only two decades, from about 1866 to 1888.

A Holy Struggle was not written in hopes of matching Hopkins' poetic voice. When writing poetry Hopkins spurted cascades of words, each one precisely chosen for its sound sense as well as its meaning. Breaking the pattern of his peers he chose not to write in regular meter, developing instead what he called "sprung rhythm" to make even the rhythm of a line closely resemble its meaning. In "The Windhover" the meter points to the image of a hawk circling in the wind:

> how he rung upon the rein of a wimpling wing
> In his ecstasy! then off, off forth on swing,
> As a skate's heel sweeps smooth on a bow-bend: the hurl
>   and gliding
> Rebuffed the big wind.

Whatever Hopkins wrote about, he marvelled at its gift of *haeccitas,* distinctiveness, something he called "inscape." Each created thing, he said, gives glory to God simply by being itself. In his poem, "The Starlight Night," admiration seems to burst through a straight channel from his heart to his pen:

> Look at the stars! look, look up at the skies!
> O look at all the fire-folk sitting in the air!

But the 1874 journal entry that precipitated this poem is calm, unrehearsed, and almost devoid of punctuation:

> As we drove home the stars came out thick: I leant back to look at them and my heart opening more than usual praised our Lord to and in whom all that beauty comes home.

The difference between the two is the distinction between the public and the private Hopkins. The tone of my sonnets is more conversational than the intense, "sprung" tone that the reader usually identifies as Hopkins'. The poems are meant to echo his private, journal voice, not to duplicate the sounds of his own poetry.

As I wrote these sonnets I asked myself, *What might Hopkins have thought and felt, had this or that happened?* A few years ago, a friend gave me Gardner's book of Hopkins' poems and prose. Whenever I leafed through it I found myself returning to a few specific entries in his journal. On August 23, 1867 Hopkins wrote:

> To the chapel of poor clares, where I made my resolution "if it is better," but now nothing is decided.

This, for Hopkins, is a straightforward, declarative sentence. But for me it seemed filled with dark hints and mysteries. I wondered, *Why* did he pray at the chapel of Poor Clares? *What* resolution did he make? *Why* is nothing now decided? It was as though I had barged in on a family discussion where the family members know one another so well, they speak in verbal shorthand. In his journal the following year, at age twenty-three, Hopkins wrote these abrupt words:

> May 2. This day, I think, I resolved.
> May 5. Cold. Resolved to become a religious.
> May 11. Dull; afternoon fine. Slaughter of the innocents.

Hopkins himself explained a little of the mystery by cross-referencing the journal entries with one another. For example, he wrote next to the May 2 entry, "See *supra* last 23rd August and *infra* May 11."

I am still curious about his visit to the chapel of the Poor Clares (uncapitalized by Hopkins). The Poor Clares are Good-Samaritan nuns of the order founded by Clare of Assisi, friend of Francis. This order is known for its charity; the Poor Clares often bring food and clothes to the poor.

I don't know what brought Hopkins to their chapel, but I believe that the resolution that he found so hard to make there was a doubly painful one: to "become a religious" against his family's will and, at the same time, to "slaughter the innocents," that is, to burn his poems.

Anyone who has studied Hopkins in school knows these two bits of his biography: he became a Jesuit; he burned his early poems. But I wondered what had transpired to make him want to destroy what he loved. Why couldn't the two occupations of poet and priest be compatible to his great, effervescent mind?

Hopkins was a kind of Renaissance man of the Victorian age. Born in 1844 at Stratford, Essex, he quickly became a likable scholar, an amateur naturalist, and an artist almost desperate to express himself.

From grade school until his death at forty-four, he sometimes allowed himself expression through various forms of art. For him the most intense form of art was, naturally, poetry. Except for one self-imposed, seven-year break, he wrote poems. But Hopkins also wrote a Platonic dialogue and part of a play. He painted, drew Blake-like illustrations, composed musical pieces, and tried his hand at the piano and violin.

Even more important to him than self-expression,

though, was sacrifice, a burnt offering of the will. Such an intense man would never be satisfied with a halfhearted dismissal of his earlier life. This young man who had become notorious at school for defying a harsh schoolmaster needed to fling up to God, in a fervid burst of flame, the one thing he loved most.

For seven years following his "slaughter of the innocents" he wrote no poetry, except for several verses requested for official occasions. Then one December day in 1875, while living in North Wales, he learned that a German ship called *The Deutschland* carrying five Franciscan nuns had been wrecked at the mouth of the Thames. (Though in my sonnets the novice from Poor Clares tells him the news, he actually read it in the *Times*.)

In *Landscape and Inscape* Peter Milward writes that as Hopkins prayed that night, he felt enormous empathy for one nun in particular, who according to the account called as she was drowning, "O Christ, Christ, come quickly!" He mentioned this account to his rector, who wisely suggested that someone should write a poem on the subject. "On this hint," Hopkins wrote in a letter, "I set to work."

Through the circumstances of a shipwreck and a rector's hint, the long-buried poetry of Hopkins burst out in experimental forms, his word choice more daring, his meter stronger and tighter than before. There in Wales, in the months preceding his ordination in late 1877, "he produced his most joyous sonnets," according to Gardner. The time that Hopkins spent cloistered without writing poems wasn't wasted, after all. It was as though he needed those seven years of silence as much as a geyser needs time to build up steam before exploding from the ground.

But life for Hopkins, even after that, was not all pied beauty and praise. As a priest and professor dedicated to hard service, he struggled to find the proper home for his poetry. He would often share his writings with his friends Robert Bridges and R. W. Dixon, but when Dixon pressed him to have the poems published, Hopkins told him that as a Jesuit he should keep himself pure, staying clear of the "dazzling attraction" of fame.

In a letter to Dixon in 1878 he wrote confidently, "The only just judge, the only just literary critic, is Christ, who prizes, is proud of, and admires, more than any man, more than the receiver himself can, the gifts of his own making."

His conviction that he should not seek fame was offset, though, by despair that his poems would never become known. In the same letter to Dixon he wrote, "It is not that I think a man is really the less happy because he has missed the renown which was his due. But still when this happens it is an evil in itself and a thing which ought not to be and that I deplore, for the good work's sake rather than the author's."

Coupled with this despair was an unspoken loneliness in the midst of frail health, frequent transfers, and long hours as college professor or parish priest. Instead of finding the Jesuit life a haven where he could reflect on "God's Grandeur," Hopkins found his duties harassing and exhausting. In a letter dated 1885 he apologized to Bridges for not writing earlier: "The long delay was due to work, worry and languishment of body and mind—which must be and will be."

The last phrase, "which must be and will be," tells more about Hopkins than he knew. "There is," Gardner wrote, "more of heroic acceptance than self pity; underneath the despair and complaint, the note of willing self-surrender to the higher necessity is always implicit." For Hopkins, the higher necessity was not his poetry but his work as a Jesuit: preaching, teaching, and living among the poor. To his Oxford friend A.W.M. Baillie he wrote from Liverpool:

I am brought face to face with the deepest poverty and misery in my district. On this theme I could write much, but it would do no good. What you write of Apuleius is interesting. But when you have a parish you can no longer read nor have intellectual interests.

In his later years as professor of classics in Dublin he completed so few poems that he complained to God in a sonnet, which he did manage to complete:

> ... birds build—but not I build; no, but strain,
> Time's eunuch, and not breed one work that wakes.

The sacrifice of his writing to his work as a university professor in Dublin could have been what engendered his last, beautiful, "terrible sonnets," so called because of Dixon's remark to Hopkins that the temper of his poetry "goes to the point of the terrible; the terrible crystal."

Hopkins' best poems were finally published, of course, though not until decades after his death. His friend Bridges brought them into print in 1918, when it seemed to him that they would be accepted by a more lenient audience than that of the Victorian age.

* * *

I never set out to write a book of sonnets on Hopkins' life, intriguing as that life is. At first I wrote only one poem, "Slaughter of the innocents," after reading again those dark journal entries of 1867 and 1868. I wrote it in his voice, in an effort to understand his thoughts that surrounded the burning of those early poems.

After writing that sonnet, I thought I was done. But instead of closing the issue I had only opened up a vein. Now there were more questions to be answered. Did he meet and talk with a novice at the chapel of Poor Clares when he prayed there, for instance? And if they continued to bump into one another at odd times, would she become a kind of muse for him, part angel, part temptation? And what would he learn from this relationship? Possibly he would discover another definition of sacrifice (literally, to "make holy") or of redemption (to "buy back.")

In the writing of these poems I found that Hopkins was becoming my true friend, a comrade-in-writing, as well as my teacher. Through his journal entries, letters, and notes I learned how he spoke of his love for the natural world, for the just-right word, and for the God who spoke them both into being. As I learned which words the man chose when speaking privately, I conjectured his reaction to imagined events in this story of a holy struggle.

I'd like to think it was God's intention that I write out these sonnets, first, for my own gradual understanding of a sacrifice of love, and second, I hope, for your pleasure in finding a soulmate in Gerard Manley Hopkins.

As kingfishers catch fire, dragonflies draw flame;
As tumbled over rim in roundy wells
Stones ring; like each tucked string tells, each hung bell's
Bow swung finds tongue to fling out broad its name;
Each mortal thing does one thing and the same:
Deals out that being indoors each one dwells;
Selves—goes itself; *myself* it speaks and spells,
Crying *What I do is me: for that I came.*

I say more: the just man justices;
Keeps grace: that keeps all his goings graces;
Acts in God's eye what in God's eye he is—
Christ—for Christ plays in ten thousand places,
Lovely in limbs, and lovely in eyes not his
To the Father through the features of men's faces.

—Gerard Manley Hopkins

PART ONE

Sacrifice

*"To the chapel of poor clares,
where I made my resolution,
'if it is better,' but now, nothing is decided."*
JOURNAL, 1867

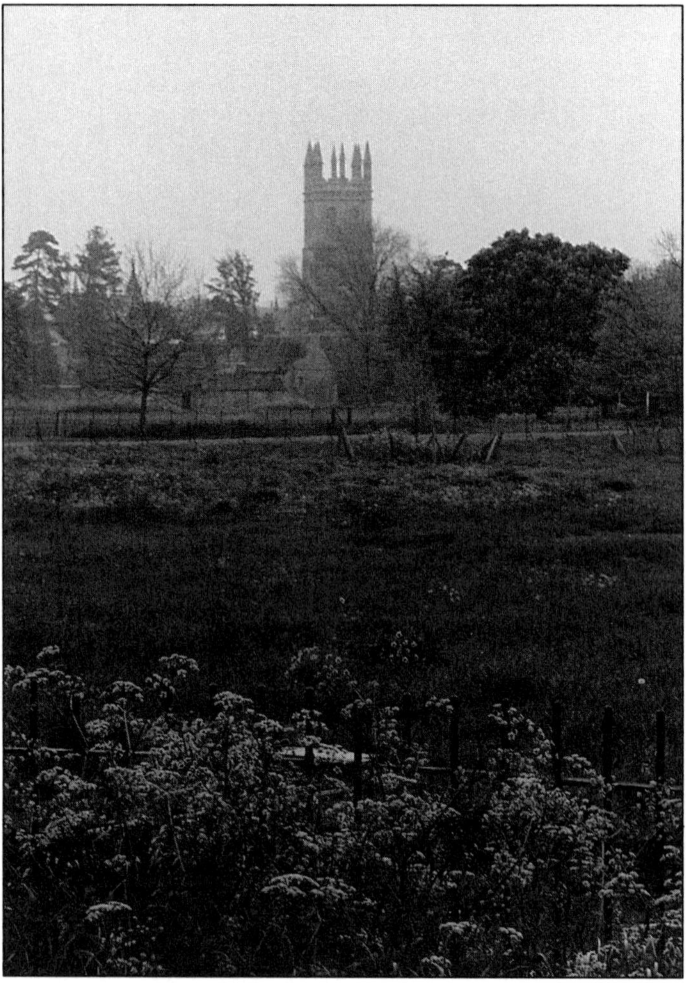

1. Unkempt

"I saw clearly the impossibility of staying in the Church of England, but resolved to say nothing to anyone...."
JOURNAL, 1866

At Christ Church, Oxford. Black swallows between
the eaves and grasses. Still the winter hangs
about, raw, unkempt. Coaching on the green
this term, besides classes. Those ragged bangs
of willows brush the green—they should be cut.
I'll make a note for the gardener. Tonight
I witnessed a rat, its eyes rabid but
its back broken, lunge at a dog and bite
its eye. I kicked the dog away and crushed
the rat's head with my heel. A ring of men
had gathered for the ghastly fight and pushed
me out into the dark, like the dog. Then
they laughed, holding up the rat. At three
tomorrow, we study Donne's poetry.

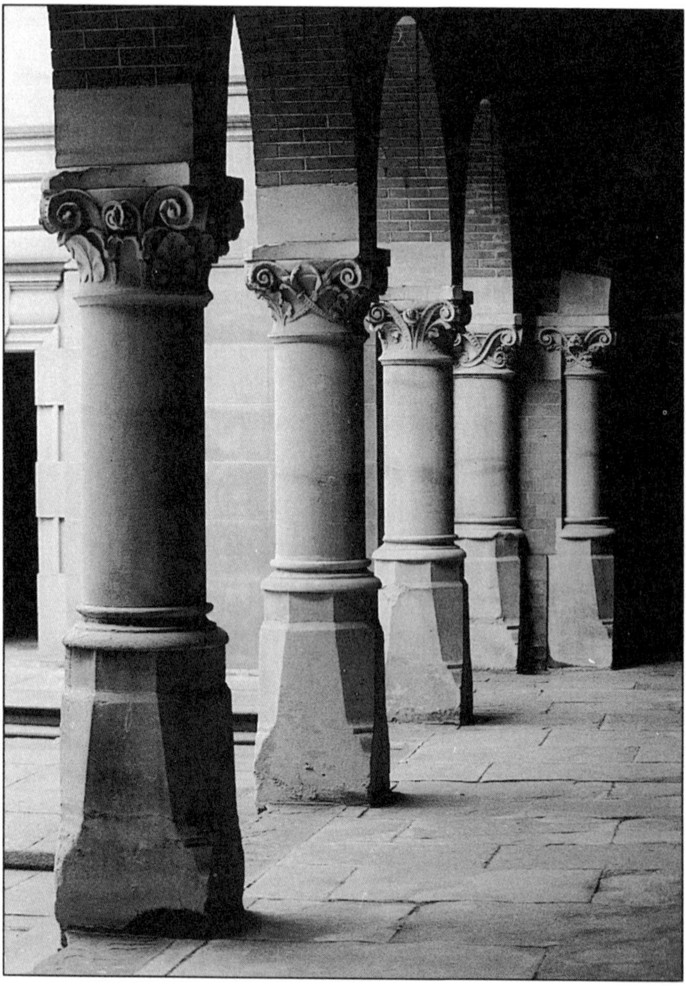

2. Plain words enough

"Some hail, which made the evening very cold, a flash of lightning, a clap of thunder."
JOURNAL, 1868

Her voice is wool, a woven scarf that wraps
my numb ears, but her eyes chill the skin—
"Oh, it's you; come in." Close thunderclaps.
The door thuds in the convent, shutting us in.

"And so. Again you've come." Plain words enough.

I follow her robe down the courtyard path.
"I had to pray once more, to know—."
                                         A cuff
from her kind hand would bless me, not the wrath
of her eyes, not the black trouble encaged
there. Ah God, I wish the cloth were light
and floated. I could show her, then, enraged
panthers in my own heart. This is the blight
of dry, ordered earth, the season of black
longing for rain. I love thee, God. Come back.

3. For the novice at poor clares

"And the world is full of things, phenomena of all sorts, that go without notice, go unwitnessed."
LETTER TO R. W. DIXON, 1878

I doubt I'll tell this word to anyone.

Not you. I'll keep it out of reverence
for whatever's hidden from the sun.

All of the singing stars, in deference
to the gold one, hum quietly all day.

Mid-ocean fills with stars, yet fails to spill.

Nightplums droop from limber trees, yet hold
(a halo rhymes the moon, more silent still)
their purple breaths, expecting to be told.

The Lord gave every dragonfly four tongues
to praise, to lip the one who caused the grey-
eyed bug to praise.
                        But Lady, this is sung
softly. It has no words, but wings, to pray.

So listen deep to what I do not say.

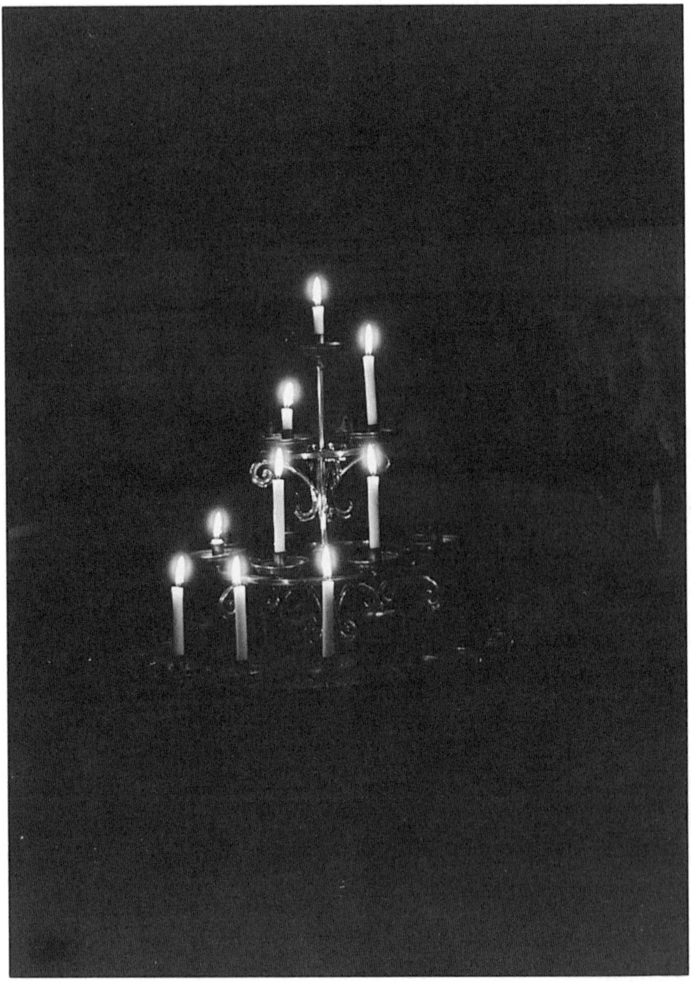

4. This cave inside me

"But if I am a priest it will cause my mother, or she says it will, great grief and this preys on my mind very much and makes the near prospect quite black."
LETTER TO A.W.M. BAILLIE, 1868

No lovewords from these flashes on the green
tonight. Cold comfort from the sparks of stars
among brick buildings. Once at thirteen
I trapped the lightning bugs in jam jars.
They seemed so fervid, though, in glassy caves,
so passionate, I had to let them go,
out through the summer dusk flaring, brave,
like ambers.
                That was a long time ago.
Now all I want is a book. I hate
this cave inside me as I walk. That black
phantom rat still craves a dwelling. Too late
I close myself. It creeps, curling its back
against my throat. Climbing the black-brick stair,
Please, I tell the library light, *be there.*

5. Which draws the world

"I have begun learning the violin. I once wanted to be a painter. But . . . the art put a strain upon the passions."
LETTER TO BAILLIE, 1868

I've taken up the violin. It seems
to scour the sooty air. I scrub the walls
with Bach, though if he heard, Johann would scream
at such outrageous strains, such caterwauls.
Had thought of painting, even found a brush
and palette. But entering the artist's shop,
I sniffed voluptuous oils. Had to rush
out, bringing the passions to a hard stop.

Music, however sensuous, appeals
to hearing, not to smell, which draws the world
of memory into the heart and keels
a poor man to his knees in penance, curled.
Though it cries like cats yammering, this
old violin is better than a kiss.

6. Juice words

"We came to fountains of the clearest black water through which pieces at the bottom gleamed white."
JOURNAL, 1868

"Shall I stay with you and pray?" she asks,
not looking at my face but at my hands.

"That would be kind," I nod, "if your day's tasks
are not too great." Insipid! She understands,
I think, that juice words like *honeysuckle,
ambrosia, nectar, passionfruit* are fine.
But a young man thirsty for God buckles
under even common words. The word *wine*
could trouble him for days; *resolve* could grieve
the man and *longing* kill him in his sleep.

"Shall I stay with you and pray?" No, leave
this pew. I cannot bear it, drinking deep,
sweet eyes, water clearer than yesterday.
If you'd help me, go to your room and pray.

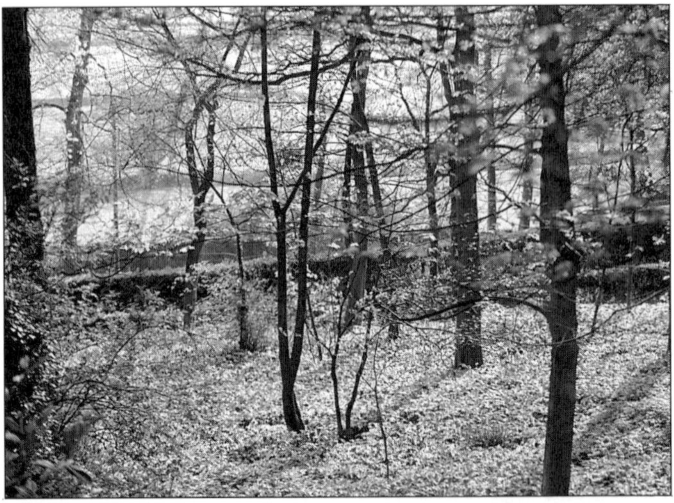

7. In certain light

"Two things as viewed by the light of each other . . . make beauty."
NOTEBOOK, 1865

A bleak dawn, as I walk here. The steam
which rises from a grey pond, with rows
of ash trees ringing it like lashes, seems
mystic this morning, prescient: "A mist rose
and watered the earth," foreshadowing flood
and judgment. The pond glitters, silver. Two
things, the pond and a woman's eye, set blood
and rivers dancing. In certain light, blue.

I am afraid of too much world. For Lent,
no puddings on Sunday. Meat but once a day.
Some tea, to stay awake. No nourishment
but bread on Ash Wednesday and Good Friday.

No more to the chapel of poor clares. She
is only flesh, and flesh is death to me.

8. Slaughter of the innocents

"May 5. Resolved to be a religious.
May 11. Slaughter of the innocents."
JOURNAL, 1868

I have no use for poems. They keep my heart
more occupied with pleated rhyme than God
(forgive me). Jesuits denounce the part
of life that most enthralls. And so, the rod
swings heavier than the pen. The sword wins.
A stroke of the blade, ten fall. No loss
is great compared to this: my self begins
again, alone, with God. Herod could toss
children on clattered cobblestones that night
for Jesus' sake, for his salvation. Why,
then, won't I burn this childish verse, a light
sacrifice indeed? Something young must die.

As poems catch fire, my heart assumes a flame
for God. Now no one will recall my name.

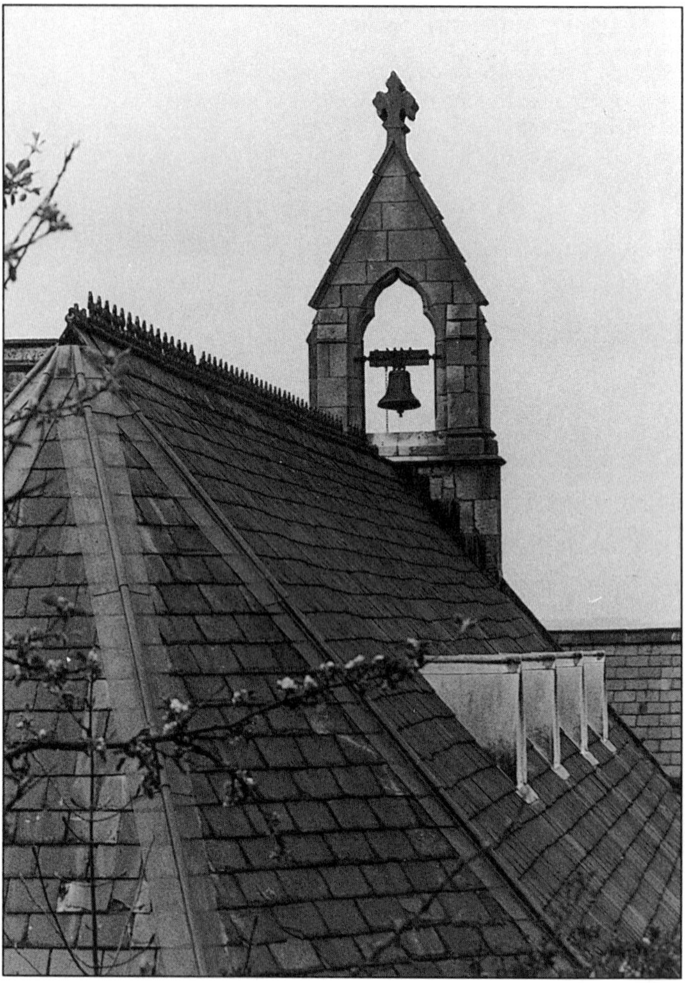

9. Pity's not an image

"Moonlight hanging or dropping on trees like blue cobweb."
JOURNAL, 1864

Winter's with us, ghost of a season. Night,
an echo of the ghost. Echoes are felt,
rather than heard, by inner ears. Moonlight
drops like tears, like white—or blue—snowmelt
from the steep roofs of chapels. No, it stalls,
as spiders drop from strings and swing there, lost
in open air like little hangmen. Falls
on whatever happens by. Felt hat, tossed
deadleaf, any hapless gnat. Savage.
                                        Stop
this whining, self. Pity's not an image.
Don't mollycoddle. Write it. Moonlight drops
on trees like blue cobweb. Better? No.
Moonlight drops like nothing. No image. So.

10. Leaping under stress

"Many beautiful works have been almost unknown and then have gained fame at last ... but many more must have been lost sight of altogether."
LETTER TO DIXON, 1878

Some nights when writing, I can lightly feel
the pen leaping under stress, inclined
to dance if I should let it. Toe, slide, heel,
but what a curious dance! Later, reclined
in bed, I dream the pen scrapes paper,
scaping stippled ink-drawn journal sketches.

The dance of paper flies, leaving vapor
in the morning, nothing. Edward fetches
me to pray, to work, to teach, to do
all manner of things but write.
                                  This is right;
I know it is. When I am grave-dropped, who
will read such chaff? What's written in the night,
a secret told myself, is shameful. Ah,
Christ, First Love, teach me not to write nor draw.

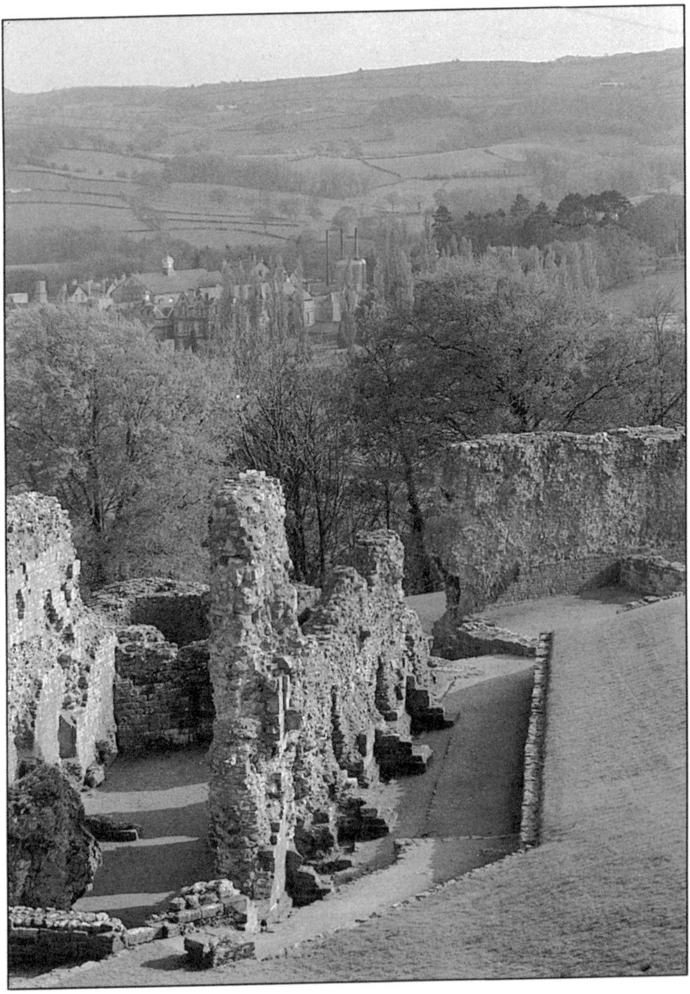

11. Kidnappers

"Looking far up the valley I felt a charm of Wales...."
JOURNAL, 1874

Chill wind. The limekiln underneath the cliff
toward Denbigh puffs white smoke; this with the grey
mist creeping on hills with sun and spindrift
give fairy-like effects. In class today
I asked Miss Jones the Welsh word for fairy.
She told me *cipenaper,* nothing more
than *kidnapper*, "to snatch away." An airy,
serious account she told me then: four
children, dressed in long frock coats and caps,
ran up and danced before her as she took
the road to Holywell. She thought perhaps
they should not be about so early, spoke
with friends: "You've seen the kidnappers," they told
her. Welsh fairy tales are real; but I am cold.

12. Not willing to go

"I want to write still as a priest, not so freely as I should have liked, e.g. nothing or little in the verse way."
LETTER TO BAILLIE, 1868

Since no one asks the whereabouts of all
those poems, I must believe that they are good
as dead—I mean that ghosts of children call
if death catches them in a rash, sprung flood
or fire and they whirl off, not willing to go.
The Welsh have heard them sobbing on the moor.
I've listened to a pack of them below
my window. Ghost children, not wolves. The poor,
ever-dying things. My poems, however,
have grieved not a soul by their absence nor
returned to mourn their own ashes. Never
will they anguish anyone anymore.
I intend to keep my journal, to do
the will of God with fire, to continue.

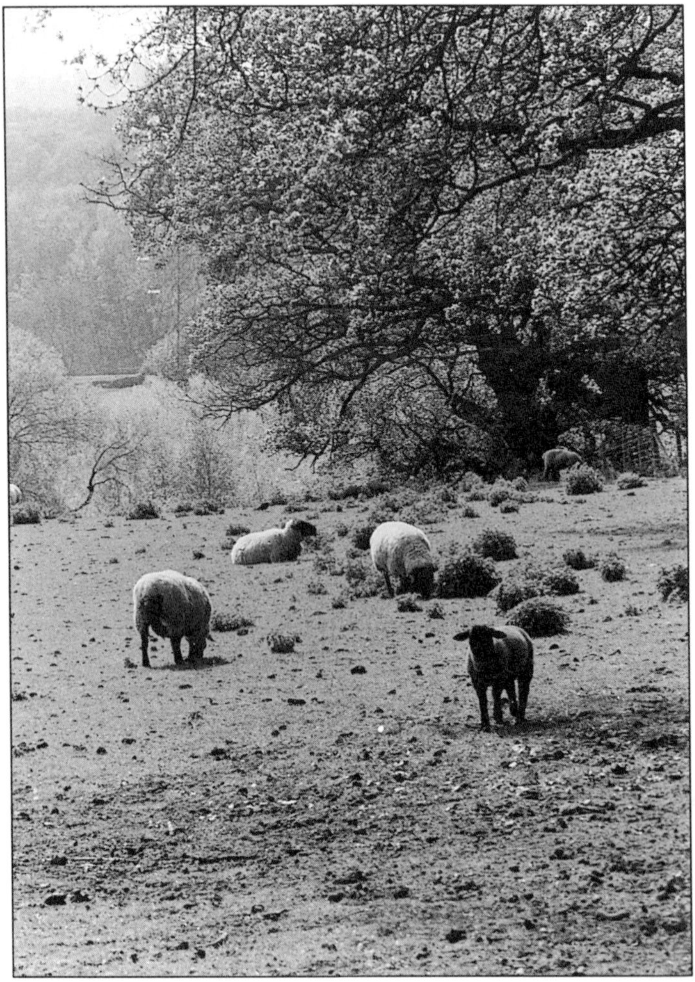

13. The air like wine

"Putting my hand up against the sky . . . I saw more richness and beauty in the blue than I had known of before."
JOURNAL, 1867

Fair; the morning fine. Some clouds look mottled,
while others speak the color white, as pure
as children's smocks. The air like wine, bottled
in blue glass. Tired . . . of what, I am not sure.

Awoke from a sound nap. The very floor
of the land was quiet, bereft of birds.
The lady from poor clares knocked at the door,
bringing bread in a basket with no words.
"Would you come in?" I asked. It sounded sharp
in such pure silence. She shook her head,
placed the bread in my hand and turned, her harp-
shaped robe billowing. I returned to bed,
unwrapped the bread and swallowed a warm, white
scrap of redemption, a small, good bite.

PART TWO

Redemption

*"This life, though it is hard,
is God's will for me
as I most intimately know,
which is more than violets
knee-deep."*
LETTER, 1881

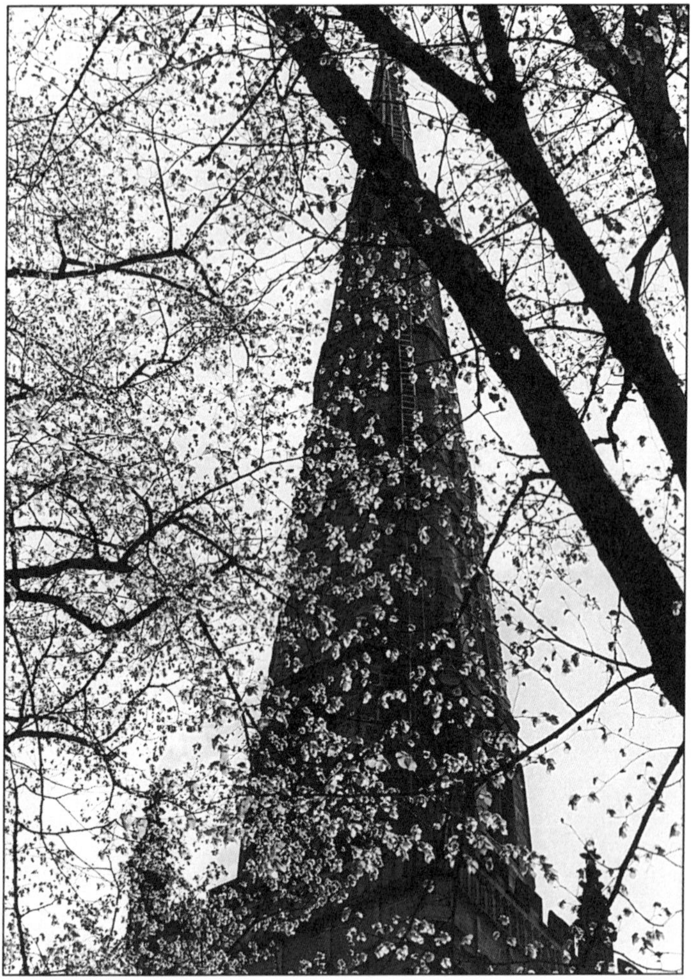

14. A jar of tulips

*"By that window what task what fingers ply,
I plod wondering."*
POEM, "THE CANDLE INDOORS"

In Switzerland, to rest. If I were strong
enough to work, I should be glad.
                                    A tall
and stately church we found to be a long
walk from the inn. With no one there at all
we stood inside, preaching to the scores
of pews. I yodelled from the organ bench.
Edward made the organ groan. The doors
opened; the rector chided us in French.

On the dark way back the chestnut leaves fanned.
A woman in her window held a jar
of tulips, a candle. Then she left, and
there was no light anywhere but the stars.

"May the good Lord shut his ears," the rector said
in French. Amen, and may he turn his head!

15. One ventures further in

"How fond of and warped to the mountains it would be easy to become!"
JOURNAL, 1868

We took a guide well up the Wylerhorn
and lunched there by the waterfall like sacks
of flour spilling. From a distance, silk-white horns
of other Alps. Close by, rocks packed like stacks
of jagged blocks. We sent away the guide;
the trail seemed clear enough. In coming down
we lost our way, had a dangerous slide
down wet, long grasses; returned to town.

Inside a glacier's grotto, the colors range
from palest blue to indigo to ink,
as one ventures further in. But a strange
reversal—lilac as one leaves, then pink.

I sketched Edward, the rocks and waterfall;
I have not written poetry at all.

16. Not the place

"But I desire . . . stones
And silence and a gulf of air."
POEM, "THE ALCHEMIST IN THE CITY"

Arose at three to climb the Breithorn, stars
of Taurus blinking edgily in sleep.
In gray twilight we tumbled over bars
of glacier ice in ragged rows, steep
moraines and sudden jaws of rock, as though
we'd caught ourselves within the frozen mouth
of the world. Its tongue was pale blue snow
until, eastward, its lips opened. Now south
in thin air we glimpse Italian peaks, gold
caps of an old man waking. Not the place
for mountain views, a summit. Clouds, the cold
boots, much talk, lunching. Even with a trace
of mankind here, what ecstasy I so
long for is swallowed, rippling down the snow.

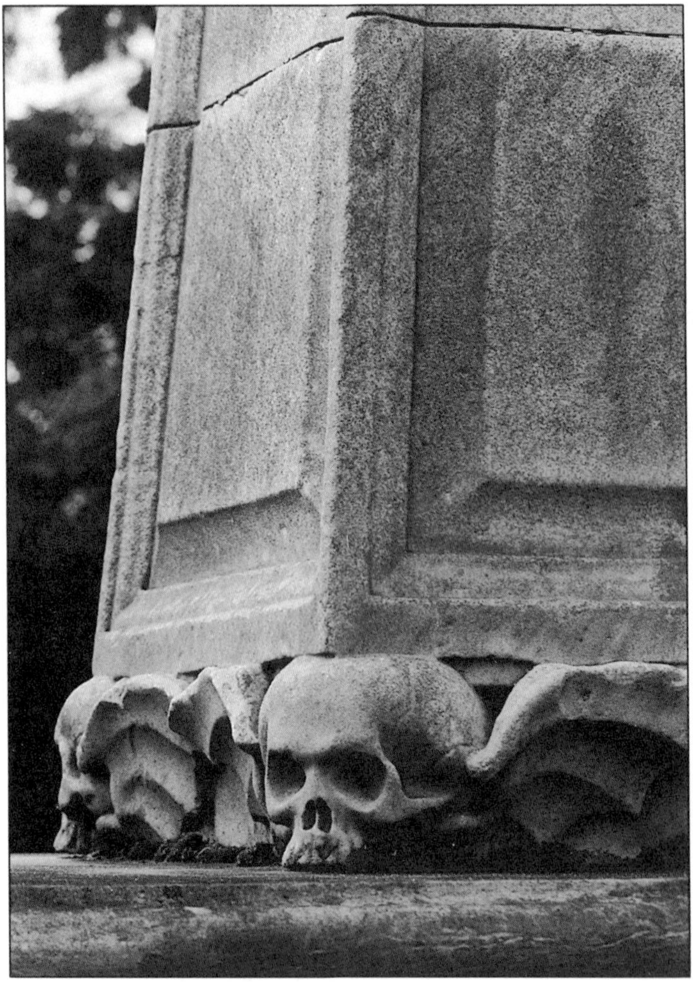

17. Agony

"There is always one touch, something striking sideways and unlooked for, which undoes resistance and pierces."
JOURNAL, 1870

Roehampton. Last night at Eucharist they read
a sister's fierce account of Christ's garden
agony. I suddenly dropped my head
and sobbed; had to beg the brothers' pardon,
scuttle out, lie here in bed, still weeping.
I could trace no cause for outburst but
the cause itself, adequate for heaping
all our grief upon.
                      A knife will cut
one's hand only if one wrenches free,
or tries, but not if one submits to pressure,
however constant or severe. For me
the story wrenched my heart by the measure
that I tore away. I think I need
holy communion, Lord, or else I bleed.

18. Prometheus

*"When will you ever, Peace, you wild wooddove . . .
Your round me roaming end?"*
POEM, "PEACE"

A poem beats its wings against my cage
as the heart bangs in fright. Not a dove
but a scavenger eagle in a rage,
screaking. I had meant to net Love
in my cunning trap. Instead, I caught a rat,
a violin, a lady, Switzerland . . .
and last, a bird of prey.
                       Now bound to that
mountain, God, because of fire I am banned
from peace and tortured in my bowels by
a poem. It sickens me, it feeds on me
insatiably, yet never lets me die!
Keep my haggard heart, Lord, stayed on thee,
Christ, Love, unbind me, kill the bird,
so I may honor thee and preach thy word.

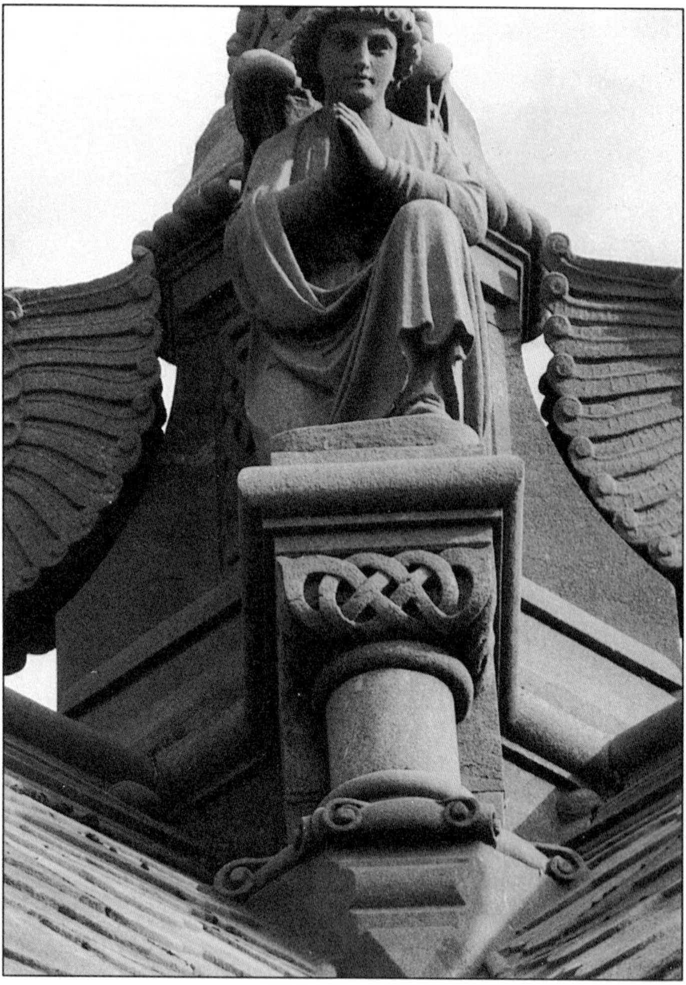

19. Turning the earth

"In a fine inspiration every beauty takes you as it were by surprise."
LETTER, 1864

In weedy ground along the chapel wall
I found a common treasure overlooked
before. In every clod, every ball
of bulb, in every shaken root and hooked
beetle gravely turning the earth I saw
the natural, unspoken manuscript
of God.
      (To find a word for, or to draw,
the thing would click open every crypt
and let the mortal ones fly up. Escape!
The word is good, but scaping *in,* precise.
To cloak oneself, to hide, in God: *inscape.)*

Crickets knew their psalms by heart. Dragonflies
inscribed God's name above stone angels, clear
wings humming, laced leaves seasoning the year.

20. Raisin cakes

"From this time I was flush with a new enthusiasm. It may come to nothing or it may be a mercy from God."
JOURNAL, 1872

The lady visited again; lovely.
Today she brought some raisin cakes and wine,
a book of mediaeval philosophy
by Duns Scotus, and her eyes. A divine
providence, I think, for I have read
half the book since tea, after she left
(for there was too much wine for one, I said)
and find this Scotus individual deft
in swaying my spirits to peace. Concrete
"thisness," as he writes . . . I have in my brain
known it but needed thisness to complete
my heart-theory of stress and scape and quain.
Peace-giver, can it be that you have sent
philosophy and eyes for nourishment?

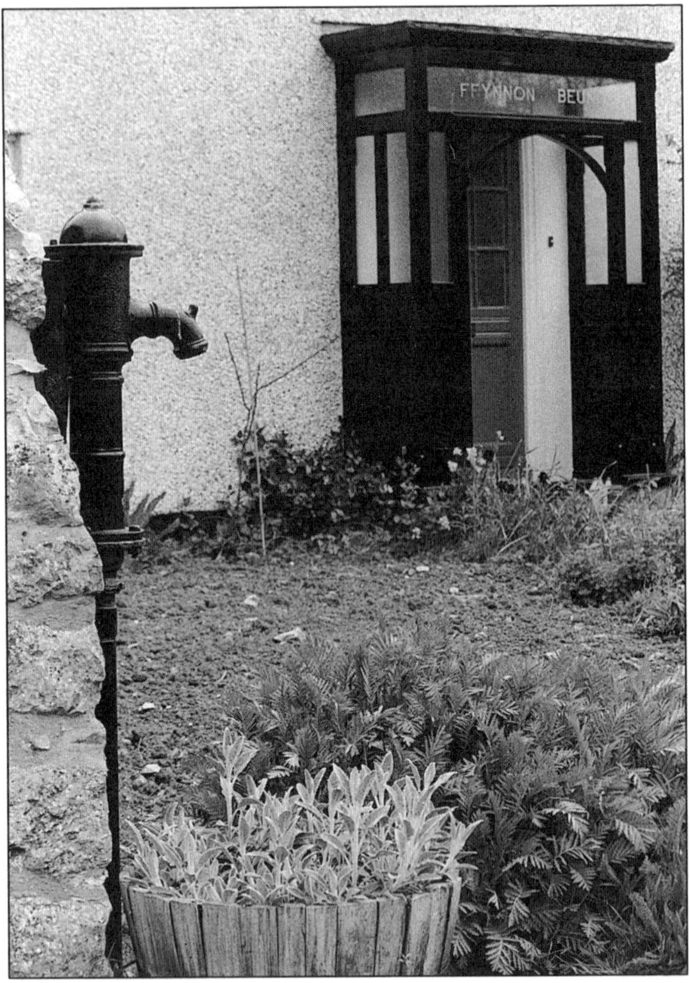
FFYNNON BEU

21. Settled for the black cloth

"I have never wavered in my vocation, but I have not lived up to it."
LETTER TO DIXON, 1881

We took a walk along the lake and chanced
to pass the chapel of poor clares. The lady
was gardening; we exchanged a few
elusive comments, then went on. Edward
asked, "Who's that? A friend? Well, what's her name?
You what? You never asked? What sort of friend
is that? Hopkins, do wake up; you're dreaming.
Where did you encounter her? How often
have you seen the girl? She *has* a powerful
stare, now, hasn't she? But it's a pity
you settled for the black cloth and she for
the habit. She can't be, Hopkins, your friend,
or what *do* you call her? If you cannot wed
the pretty girl, then write a damned poem!"

22. The lady's eyes

"Beauty—dangerous; does set dancing blood."
POEM, "TO WHAT SERVES MORTAL BEAUTY?"

I love the lady's violent eyes, dark
as clovestars, crying pools in echo wells.
Her cry: *Go on.* Ambiguous bark
that may mean *speak* or *leave.* No one tells.

I love the lady, love the lady's eyes.
A ripe acorn, suspended from the lip
of an oak leaf cluster, drops, and it dies.
Squirrels forage for it, but only the tip
is visible, and this the leaves smother.
No sapling grows there, gracing the old earth.
No scroll is planed, no cradle for the mother
from the oakwood that is not.
                              In your birth,
Lady, your eyes began to guard my breath.
They dance between my bones and keep my death.

23. Blue behind the veil

"I thought how sadly beauty of inscape was unknown and buried away from simple people and yet how near at hand it was."
JOURNAL, 1872

Hard frost, bright sun, a sky of blue ocean.
Here at the Isle of Man the waves are draped
in linen, rolled like bread dough. Such a motion
charms the eye. All morning I have scaped
the harp-strung breakers—white at the crest,
intensely blue behind the veil. To see
the dance of feather waves within a nest
of rocks is restful. I remember she
had offered me a feather as we talked
outside the convent. Edward stared at it
as though it were a knife; and then we walked
on. I feel its softness in my pocket.
My penance, God: I must find thee in place
of her and never touch her Christlike face.

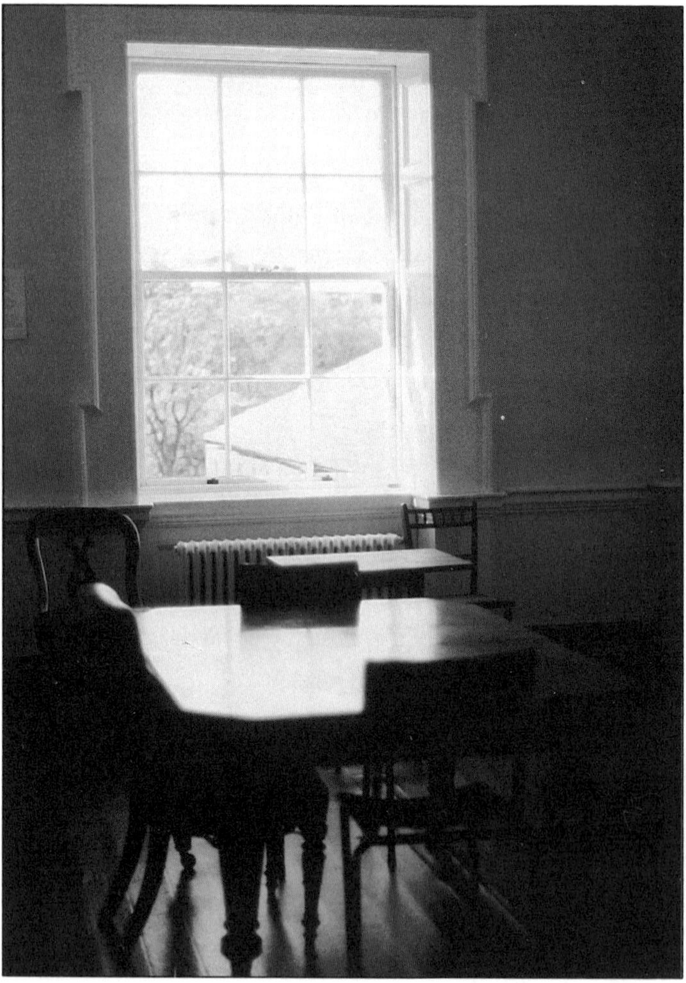

24. The sea rain

"Altogether perhaps my heart has never been so burdened and cast down as this year. But in all this our Lord goes His own way."
JOURNAL, 1874

At dawn we sailed for Liverpool. Before
we left I looked long at the clay waves,
as carved as cliffs they hurl against, each core
exploding white and jagged. Next behaves
as last, like sacrificial ranks of sheep
to slaughter, score on score, or not-at-fault
swine swallowing evil, thrashing at steep
cliffs, recoiling.
            I think it is the salt
that makes the sea rain sting so much. A stern-
eyed, handsome boy on board got drunk and sang
"I want to go home, go home." From Blackburn
port we slogged through sloppy fields. Clouds hang
exhausted from these hills at dusk, unable
to rise. I must find candles for the table.

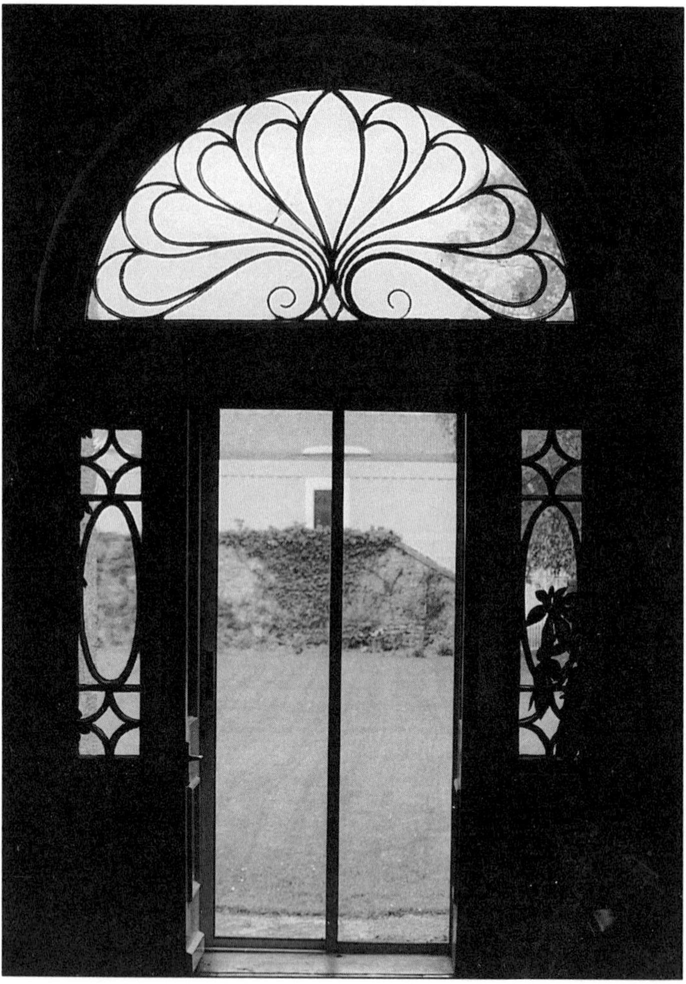

25. The mystery of Grace

*"And what is Earth's eye, tongue, or heart else, where
Else, but in dear and dogged man?—Ah, the heir
to his own selfbent so bound."*
POEM, "RIBBLESDALE"

By men's minds my heart, my eyes so much
are bound that I forget a woman's heart
is bound by bones alone. A rabbit hutch
of ribs enthralls it.
                *Four thousand equal parts,
quite markedly symmetrical. Just so.
Quite right. Ahem. What did you say? The tea,
sir. Ah yes, the tea.* And so it goes,
in drawing rooms of men.
                Christ, where is she?
I hold her eyes in mind. Ah, no. I must
be mindful that a woman's eyes embrace
a poor man tighter than a snake. I trust
the mystery of Grace will not erase
my memory of holy love but bind
me to my dearest Heart, or I be blind.

26. A lost one

"This skeleton inscape of a spray-end of ash is worth noticing for the suggested globe: it is leaf on the left and keys on the right."
JOURNAL, 1872

The ashtree growing by the garden fence
was felled. I heard the wild geese go by,
then *scrape-throat* like a lost one trailing: tense,
impassioned shrieks as none on earth could cry.
It was the saw, lopping limbs. I turned
inside and wished to die, not hear the groans
of ash falling, inscape to be burned.

First saw the Northern Lights, upwhirling cones
of smoke-pink signal fires. They seem to drift,
not following the warp of earth but free
of it—a bee swarm, charm of swallows, rift
in mist from flaring waves—but simply . . . to be
preoccupied with heaven, to be thrilled
with, ah, delightful fear—not felled but filled.

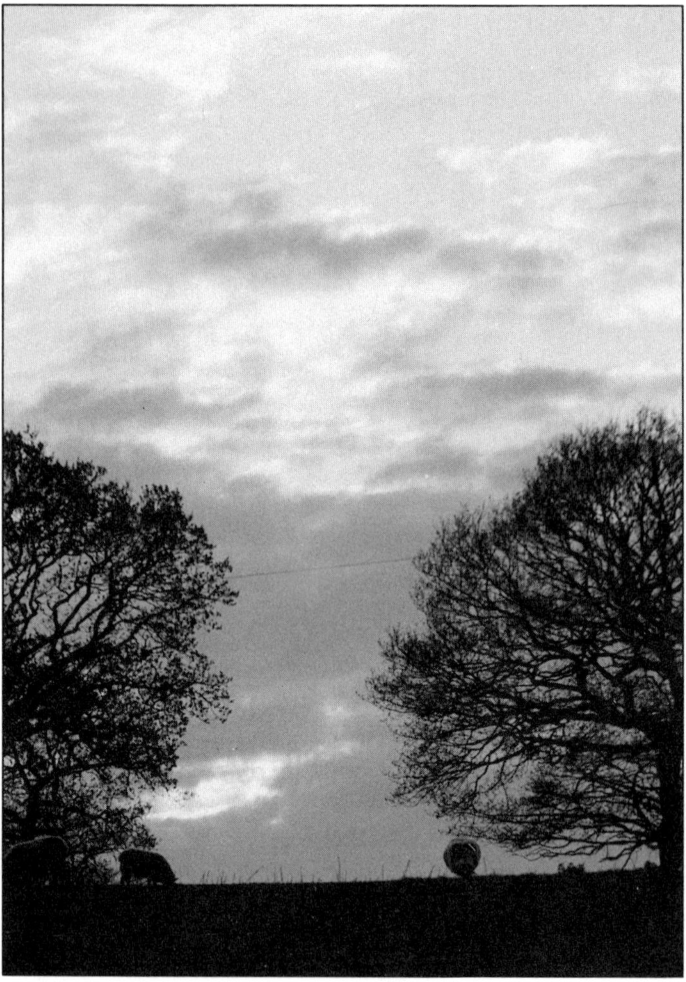

27. Bleed beauty

"The other side of the valley shewed a hard and beautifully detached and glimmering brim against the light, which was lifting there."
JOURNAL, 1874

Again across the field she visited,
this time with eyes like pewter suns
and news of death. While I stood riveted
she told me of the five Franciscan nuns
who drowned just outside the mouth of the Thames.
The Deutschland wrecked in storm-swirls of snow, one
sacrifice of five exiles, five gems
floating down to bleed beauty to no one.

"Christ deliver them," I murmured. What more
could she want wrung from such a preacher? A long
look, hard and fever-bright, then out the door.

If I began to spill my heart's red song,
I would not stop—my heart's pang, shiver,
long fire, I could not stop—my heart's blood river . . .

28. Seven years

"I was affected by the account, and happening to say so to my rector, he said he wished that someone would write a poem on the subject. On this hint I set to work..."
LETTER TO DIXON, 1878

Lady, Grace, what is not spoken of—
though wildly sung through veins from the heart's rim—
is blood of the beloved, holy love.
What have we spoken, these seven slim
years, to one another? A silent vow,
as when bodies pass the Body, we took
at first blush. Except for greetings now
and again, we seem as quiet as a book.

But when you came to me, piercing your heart
for your sisters, what bright language your body
spilled! These seven years I have lived apart,
to kill the passions. But now may God
be with us as we speak. May grace be bread
for us. And may our love be still unsaid.

PART THREE

Another sacrifice

*"But I did aim at two things
not in themselves unattainable,
if to me far easier things
were not now unattainable.
But of these, if ever, hereafter."*
LETTER TO BRIDGES, 1885

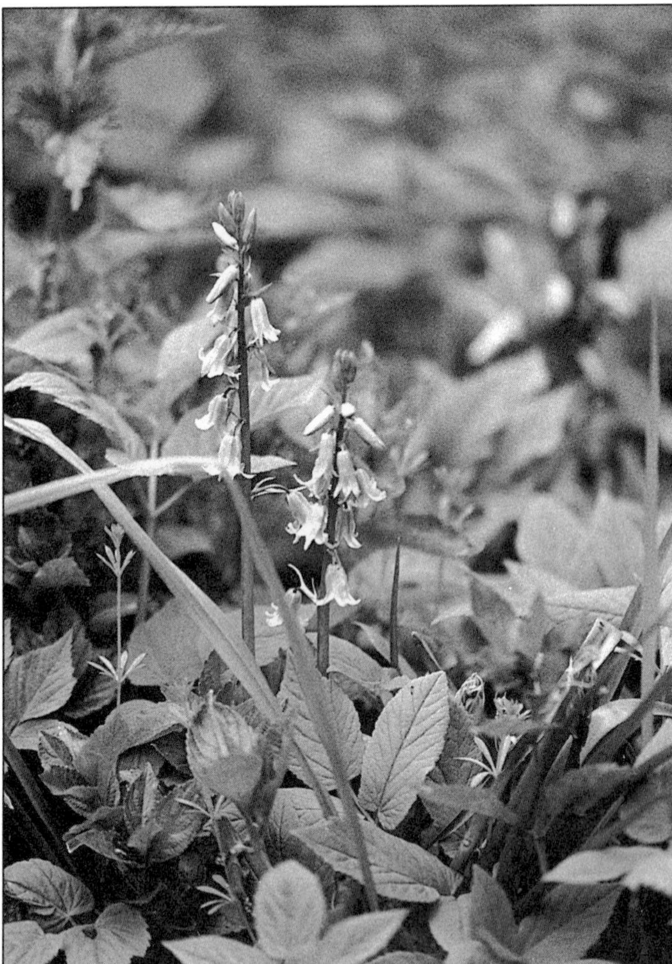

29. Bluebell

"All things . . . are charged with love, are charged with God and if we know how to touch them give off sparks and take fire."
NOTEBOOK, 1881

No other flower than the bluebell, striking
in a field, calls God's great character
so painfully. It baffles every sense,
kindles inscape. From this little hill run
falls of sky-born blooms. I choose the brightest
one, fitting my fingertips in thimble
stalls. Rubbed against my cheek it murmurs
honey smells, jostles like the sound of wings.
On my tongue, a sweet gum when I bite it.
Candleblue, shepherd staff, wind instrument
drawn out with God's own breath and elegant
hand. Kingfisher blue bloom sparks catching
fieldfire race all aflame downhill,
yield wellwater, ring and tell of him.

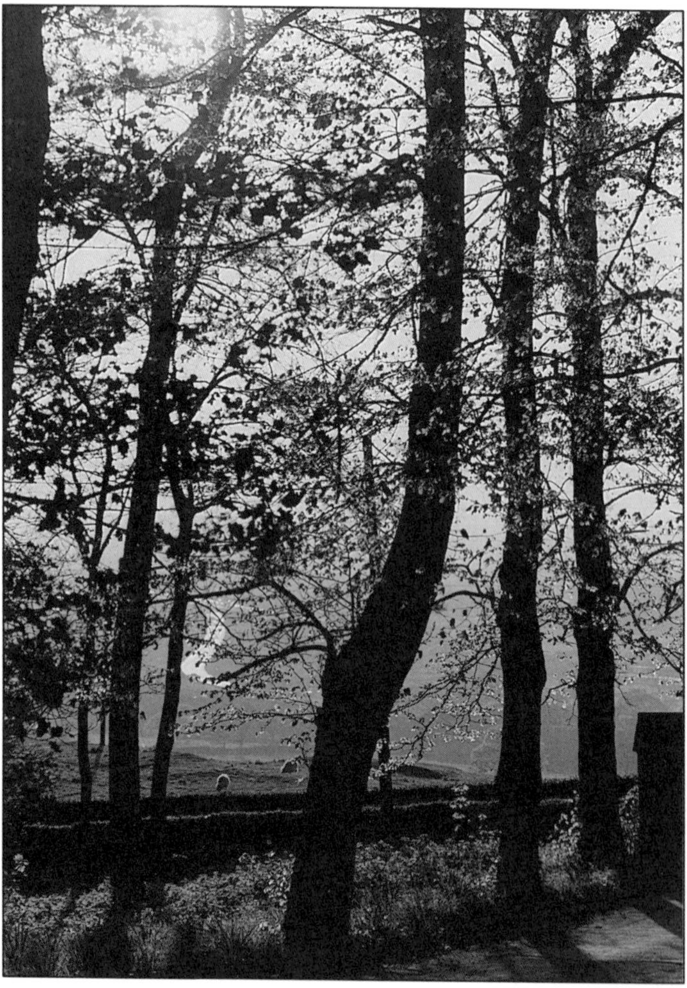

30. This pure world

*"A strain of the earth's sweet being in the beginning
In Eden garden."*
POEM, "SPRING"

When light spreads butter-yellow on the lake
and bronze birds trill in the garden as though
this pure world were a genesis, I take
a walk, no thought of her. The light will go
as clear as bellsong, allowing earth to be
its own evanescent color at noon.
Birds fall mute, as brothers thoughtfully
move about the grounds in prayer. Soon
the late sun burnishes the chapel lawn;
birds recall the bells with sacred twitter.
At dusk I never think of her, sun gone,
birds escaping into sky turned bitter
plum. I never listen for a furtive tread
upon the stair and never miss her in my bed.

31. At zenith

"I have desired to go
Where springs not fail,
To fields where flies no sharp and sided hail
And a few lilies blow."
POEM, "HEAVEN-HAVEN: A NUN TAKES THE VEIL"

At dawn the rarest sky arched over me.
I scaped its blue cut stones, inwoven veins
of gold. At zenith, lapis lazuli
fitted, as a capstone. Packed with quains
and margaretting so that all the sky
was like a crystal, tight and fire-shining,
sapphire cut my eye, a doorway.
                                         High
off I sit and read, the moon declining.

The riverbank slopes quickly from this hill.

The water sounds like children. Say the moon
has eyes and watches both of us.
                                      A still
morning—over my head a road stretches,

yawning, I find it hard to keep my eyes

from closing on this page

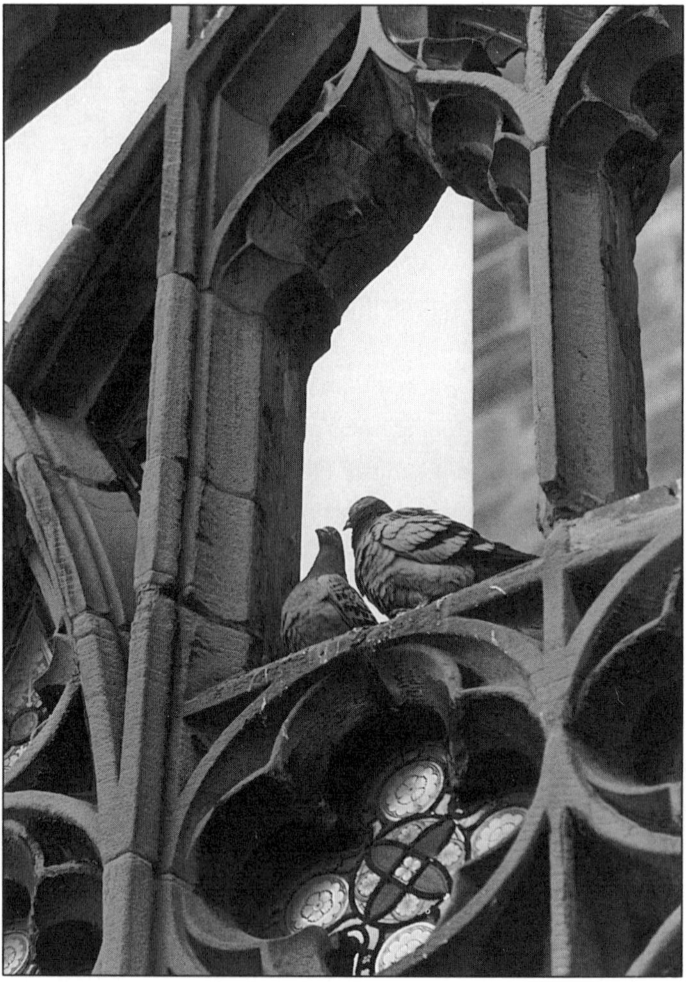

32. A wet flaming

*"The extreme delight I felt when I read 'Her eyes like lilies shaken
by the bees' was more than any single line in poetry ever gave me."*
LETTER TO DIXON, 1878

The morning fair and cloudless, Grace
appeared with biscuits, a kindness. We fed
the crumbs to pigeons on a wooded trace
behind the church. She pointed out their red-
stockinged feet, one with thundercolor wing
and one with purple cuttleshells. One bird
betrayed a satin crush of green. Turning
its neck, a wet flaming. At times we heard
the cuckoo's sharp and fluty notes; hollows
hold them till they spring, spurting with alarms.
The fields were full of lilies, blue swallows
at dusk, and lambs. Grace held one in her arms.

Without her kind comradeship I would miss
beauty. But kindness can be dangerous.

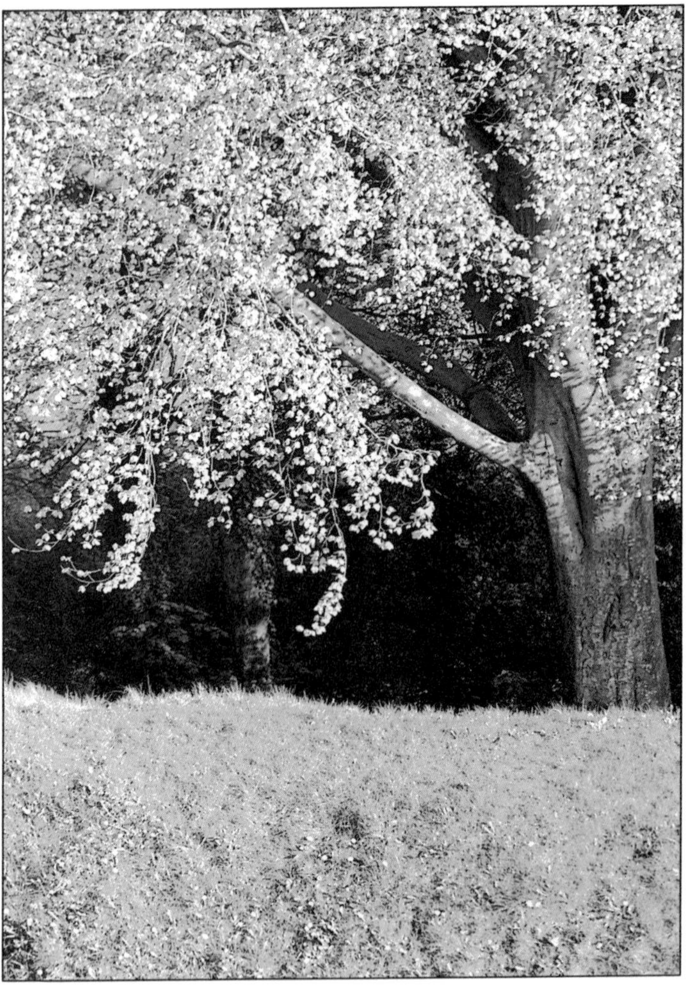

33. Clair-obscure

"Leaves, like the things of man, you
With your fresh thoughts care for, can you?"
POEM, "SPRING AND FALL"

Quite hot; the south wind dappling my face
as I came out, though, seemed to dress me all
in linen or in shadow. I spoke with Grace
about the clair-obscure in 'Spring and Fall,'
a "woodcut poem," she called it. But if grief
can chill young Margaret, God knows what will be
our colder darkness.
                      "Turn the leaf,"
she said; "it blackens or blanches. Our Tree
dances; Christ is all a dance."
                              If I tell
her how my soul has craved such talk, I may
cause shadows. Poor Clare, I love you well
in this great heat of poetry. Please stay.

To speak it brings the thing to light. Too weak,
I cannot make it so. I cannot speak.

34. Holy company

"When one mixes with the world and meets on every side its secret solicitations, to live by faith is very hard. . . ."
LETTER TO DIXON, 1881

The Lord God said in Eden, "Every tree
is good, the garden round with goodness. Yet,
a certain central tree is not for thee."
A wide, inviting circle like a net
he cast upon the wilderness: a walled
garden gracefully enclosing two
small fish. Not with a hook or gaff he called
us to himself. Without a spear he drew
us in, but with a net of love. We came
to him for food and holy company.
Then God, the fisherman, cut short the game
and hauled us out, gasping for the sea.

Why did he tell us, Every tree but one!
Knowing *that* is the one we want. That one.

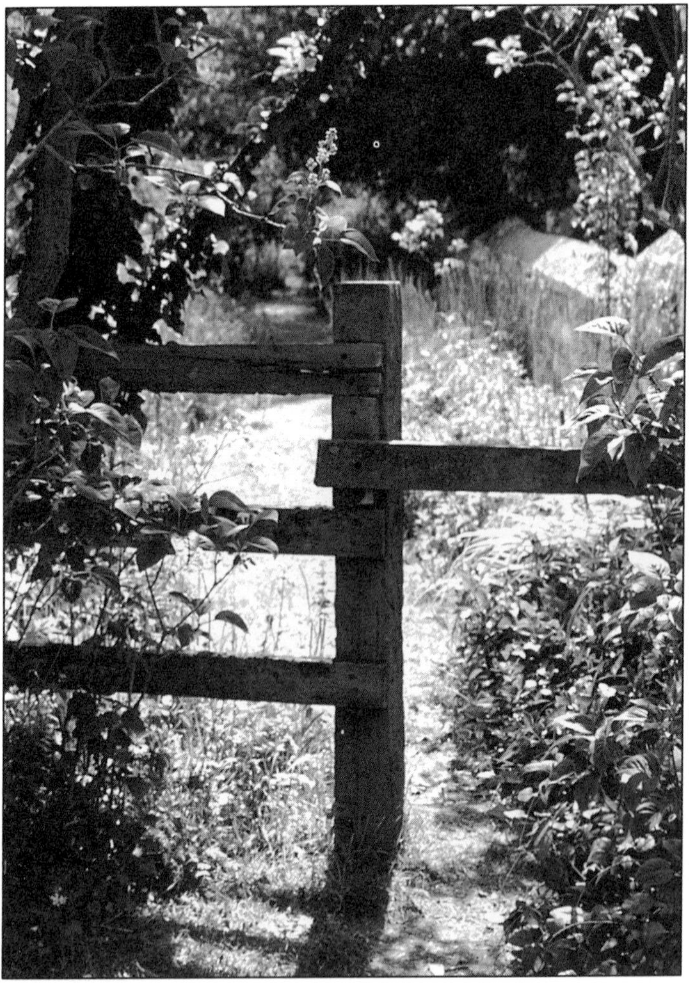

35. Languishing

"Feeling, love in particular, is the great moving power and spring of verse and the only person that I am in love with seldom stirs my heart sensibly..."
LETTER TO BRIDGES, 1879

From an aching storehouse, my barn bursting
to give, I fling out bales of poetry
and spread them as a bed for her. Thirsting
for reply, I wait.
                    Gracefully she
leans, pouring out her praise like water,
lips a flagon spout, words releasing words
my swollen throat languishing hotter
drinks.
           But to spill my self to her as birds
blurt their personal song to blossom sky
would be a mortal crime against the Lord
and all the rules of St. Ignatius; I
should gather up the bales again and hoard
them all, for Christ. "Though the fig tree shall
not blossom, and there be no herd in the stalls...."

36. No relief

"I held myself free to compose, but cannot find it in my conscience to spend time upon it; so I have done little and shall do less."
LETTER TO DIXON, 1878

This love is badly listing. I cannot right
it, bail, add ballast or throw overboard
some needful thing. ─────────

───────────── Wrecked on a reef
by a warm zephyr, unexpectedly
pressed to one another, no relief
on any parched horizon, ─────────.

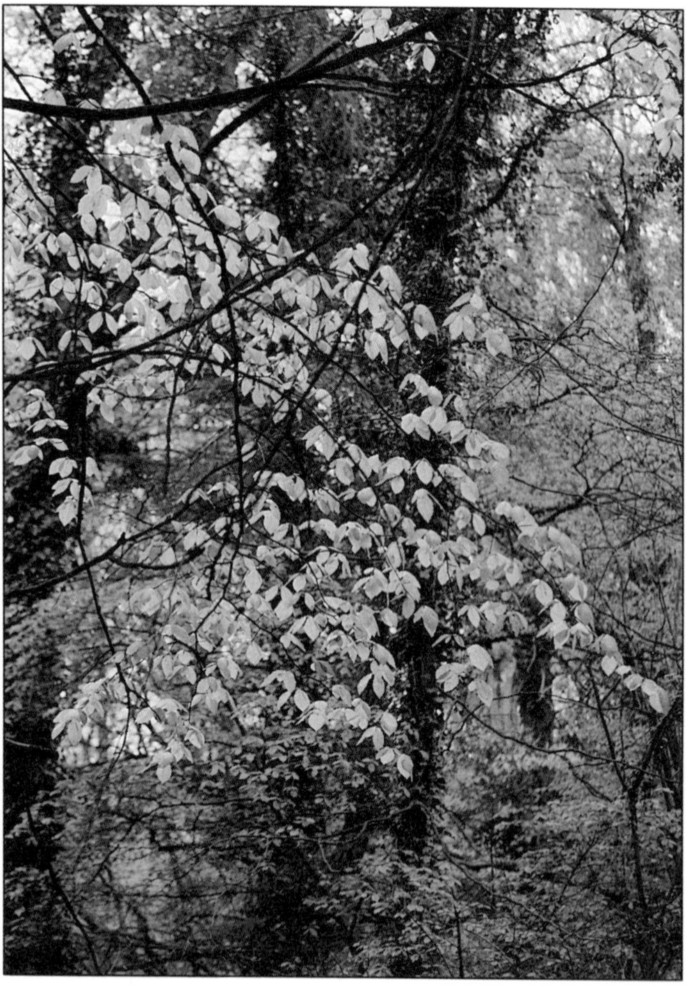

37. Fugue

"Make believe
We are leafwhelmed somewhere...."
UNFINISHED POEM, "EPITHALAMION"

We lay beneath a thatch of tanglewood
not far from chapel bells, each gong longer
than the last. To give account we should
have left the bronze woods. But the woods were stronger.

And though we spoke alone, it seemed a three-
part fugue. "I fear this love—" I told her.

"—But you are not afraid of love."
                                     "Not really?"

"Not afraid of love, but of something colder:
its counterfeit."
                   "Aha. And what is that?"

"You know," she said; "lust of the eyes. You love
so well so many things—music, the flat
crest of clouds on the horizon above
the dawn, and you love me. Yes, me," she said.

At dawn I wakened in my narrow bed.

38. Revelation

"I do not think I can be long here; I have been long nowhere yet."
LETTER TO BAILLIE, 1880

How long I slept! How long *did* I sleep?
Edward, good brother, found me in the hills
and brought me home like a lost, tired sheep.
I dreamed of flight. Suppose the whippoorwills
exchanging love notes caused my dreams, or birds
whose names I could not know, feather-strange,
beguiled me with their haunting, ardent words
while I slept. Nothing indistinct will change
back, *selve*, become itself again. The dreams
are clouds. In revelation, though, I flew.
That much I know. I know I saw the cedar beams
of Heaven's roof, not far from here, and true.

I know that Christ, who seems, like ladies' charms,
so distant, brought me home in Edward's arms.

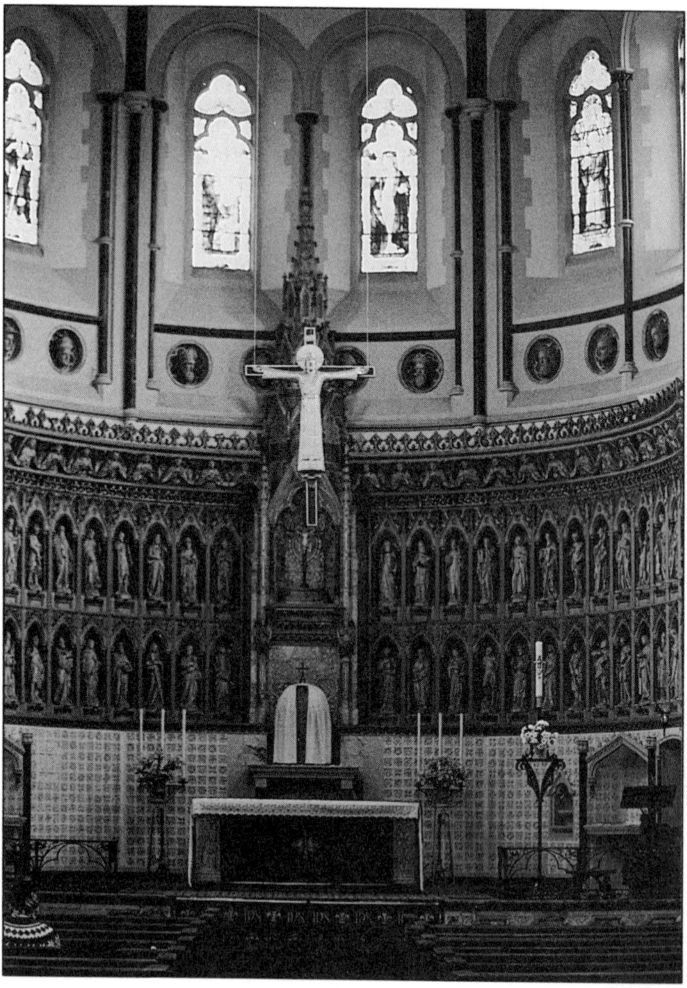

39. Beside me empty

I hear confessions, preach, and so forth; I have still a good deal of time to myself, but I find I can do very little with it."
LETTER TO DIXON, 1878

At least I say my work in Liverpool
harasses and makes writing hard. Tonight
in my confessional I sit, the stool
beside me empty. To my absurd delight
the faithful few have been reduced to none;
my sermon unexpectedly will fall
upon deaf ears, undone. Here comes someone.

Christ have mercy; the lady. Why, of all
evenings to be dispossessed of a crowd
of witnesses, should Grace appear at my
black booth?
         "Bless me, Father—" she says aloud,
then sits in darkness with a holy cry
that tells me nothing.
         "Go in peace," I say;
"God keep your heart in his." She walks away.

40. A lovely creature

"I think that my fits of sadness, though they do not affect my judgment, resemble madness. Change is the only relief, and that I can seldom get."
LETTER TO BRIDGES, 1885

A visitor at church this morning blew
in black as a matchstick burnt, a fine ash
powdering his back, his leggings yellow. Who
invited such a lovely creature? Sash
wide I hoped he'd find his own way out
without my forcing. Instead he perched up in
the gallery, lamenting loud about
my sermon. Such an unrepentant din
he made that three church elders tried, and failed,
to dislodge the character. At offering
and prayer all was silent as a nailed
coffin but for the fluttering of wings.

Christ, my darling
Lord, a starling.

41. In orchards not kept

"Complete thy creature dear O where it fails,
Being mighty a master, being a father and fond."
POEM, "IN THE VALLEY OF THE ELWY"

From the great shadow a fall apple fell
in my palm, red-brown like a maple leaf.
Heavy, unpolished like rose quartz, it was hell
in hand, bearing an old name for old grief.

I carried around the death of Christ, held
his curled body red-brown against my ribs
whispering "Forgive me, Father," smelled
in orchards not kept
               (O taste and see
that the Lord is good.) All was for an apple,
an apple I took falling from an old tree.

But the ruddy skin had tricked. Bruises dappled
the soft flesh. My God, the whole orchard hung
with fruit this sweet, this agonized, this young.

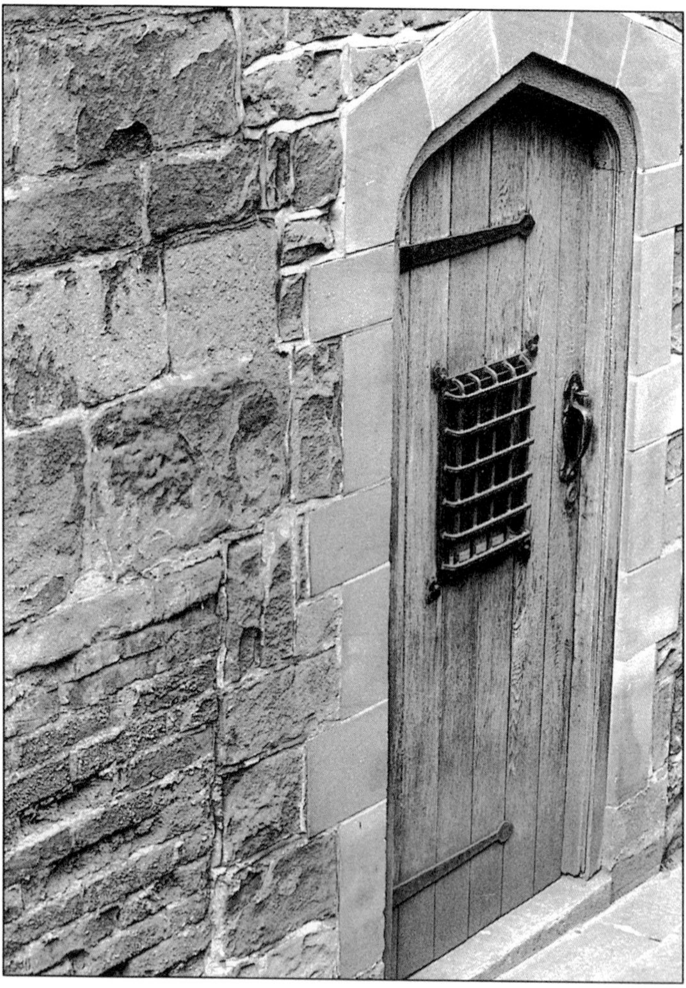

42. Cloistered

"Sweet fire, the sire of muse, my soul needs this;
I want the one rapture of an inspiration."
POEM, "TO R.B."

After several months of silence I made
a journey home to speak with Grace once more.
At the convent Sister Caroline stayed
me with a look, then firmly shut the door.

"What is it?" she demanded.
                    "I came
to visit Grace, to show her these little
fragments of poems. She might help me tame
them into sonnets."
                    Her voice was brittle:
"Grace is cloistered. She is praying now."

"Well, when she comes out, then—" I began,
but Caroline said, "No."
                    "If not, then how
could I convey these to her?"
                    "As a man,"
she said, "you may not ever speak with Grace
again."

Now nothing's left, Lord, but disgrace.

43. Keep Grace

"We compose fragmentarily...."
LETTER TO BRIDGES, 1885

If I cannot keep Grace, let me lift,
let her go to thee.
                      But Christ, keep *me*
in Grace, forgetting doubt and shift
and turnabout.
                      No, God. Keep Grace in me
and thee.

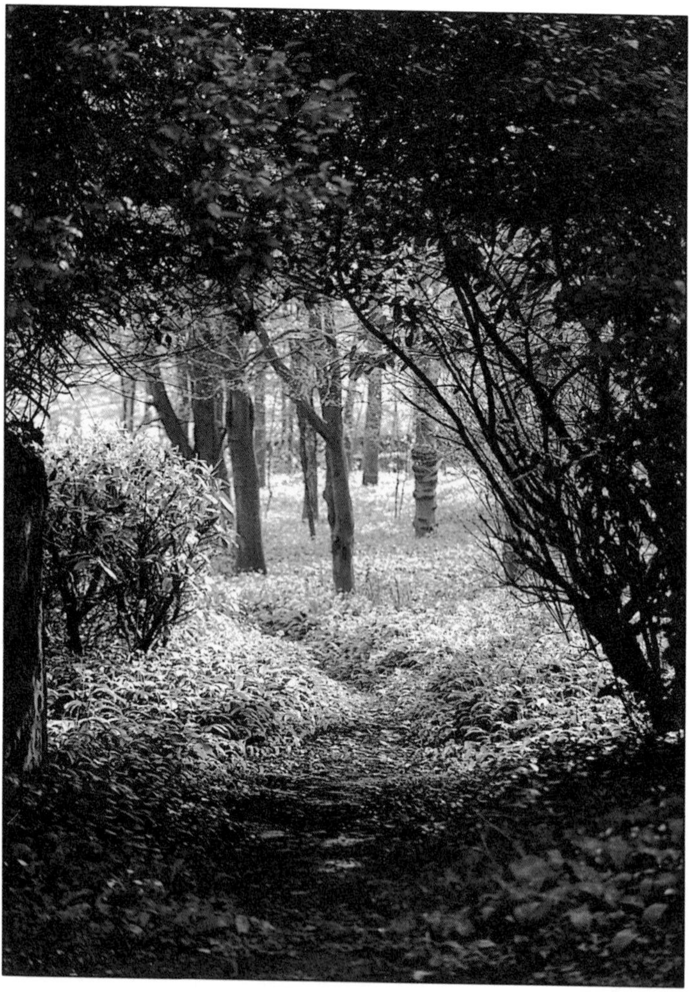

44. A sad and holy struggle

"This is enough for the time...."
LETTER TO BRIDGES, 1888

The bliss, a poem is, of being born,
coupled with extraordinary tension,
which is dying. One is forever torn
from another. But hush, never mention
this; too dangerous. A poem recalls
the pain of birth, which is the birth of pain,
a sad and holy struggle. Death befalls
us all, Amen. Yet turn the leaf again.
The birth, a poem is, of death, and still
the death of it. Such longing cannot be
for long. Mortal struggles either kill
or heal. Calamities bring some degree
of pathos to a poem. While death delays,
a fearful poet's heart is rinsed with praise.

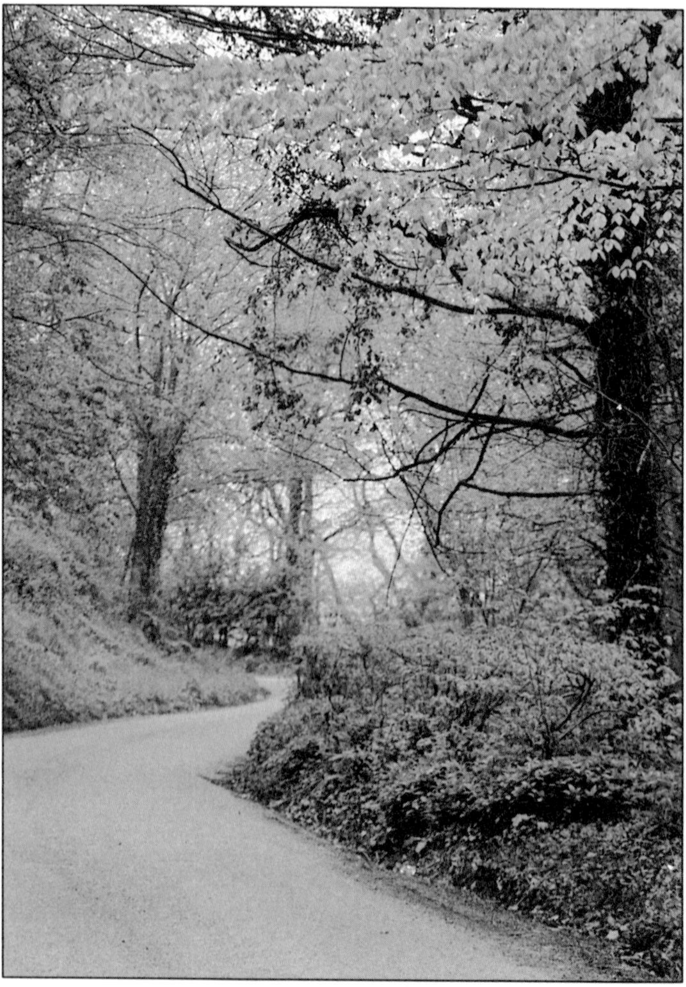

SCRAPBOOK

In May 1991, one hundred and two years after Gerard Manley Hopkins' death, Luci Shaw and I followed the path of Hopkins' life, travelling from London to Dublin and back. We took that path, as Luci wrote then in her journal, "not just for a practical photojournalism assignment but for a feeding of mind and spirit, a re-freshment, re-creation." On the following pages we have put together a scrapbook of the journey, with photographs and journal entries arranged to reflect the chronology of Hopkins' life.

All along the way, like white stones dropped in the forest, we found kind people who knew and loved Hopkins' writings. They led us through the same gardens and rooms where Hopkins had written, prayed, studied, and preached. We were given impromptu tours by a variety of guides: Michael Bampton, a retired professor at Manresa house; Father Paul Edwards, a Jesuit priest at St. Beuno's Retreat Center; Sister Margaret, who serves meals at the medieval hostel by St. Winefred's Well; Richard O'Rourke, a County Kildare chemist and Vice-President of the International Hopkins Society; and Allen Tadiello, Assistant Librarian at Balliol College, Oxford.

Though we had no way of contacting these kind guides beforehand, they did not seem a bit surprised that we had shown up on their doorsteps unannounced. Not that people come every day to ask about the poet. Father Edwards, who is the Hopkins aficionado at the remote St. Beuno's, told us that he had lived there off and on since the 1930s, yet he had never been visited by Hopkins researchers before. Our thanks to those who gave us much more than information for this book.

London: In 1844, Hopkins was born at Stratford in Essex. Eight years later he and his family moved not far away, to Oak Hill Park on Hampstead Hill overlooking London. As an adult, he often returned to his parents' home there.

We took the train and underground into London to Hampstead and walked uphill to find Gerard Manley Hopkins' boyhood home at Oak Hill Park. Looked for his house, #9, but nearly all homes on this street have been demolished and replaced with blocks of flats. One building tenant showed us an oak tree where the Hopkins' home had been.—L.S.

The tenant, an old woman, told us she knew "quite a lot about Hopkins," but that "there's been quite a lot of books already published on him," if we wanted to read them, and she was hoping that we were the doctor she was expecting. Ohh.—M.S.

Oxford, England: In 1863, Hopkins entered Oxford University, Balliol College. As a senior undergrad, he probably occupied these rooms overlooking Fellows Green.

Walked up to Balliol College. At the gate office the sign said "Open to the Public 2-5." It was 5:30. The man looked on us pityingly and said, "Only the two of you? Go on into the quad." Across the green we could hear singing. A chalkboard sign in another entrance said "Evensong 5:30—All Welcome," so we slipped in to a back seat up high, next to a tall severe looking man in a black robe with white eyelet ruffles. He pushed a hymnal at us, and we joined in. Afterwards, the cleric invited everyone for sherry in the common room. The man in the black robe took it off and became quite human, welcoming us. Someone in English Lit. was directed our way to talk to us about Hopkins as requested. Jean Grace Craig, with a strong Scots accent, supplied us with torrents of information and pointed out GMH's ground floor window, now the Junior Commons Room.

Today, a long walk up to New Inn Hall St. to look for #18 where GMH had had rooms his first year of college, but it was not. Only an old wall left, surmounted by a modern glass/steel office building. On to St. Aloysius Catholic Church, where GMH had been on staff 1878-79. To Binsey a few miles away, verges and fields full of yarrow. With great courage, Marg took the narrow, winding road past signs saying NO PARKING BEYOND THIS POINT, RESIDENTS ONLY, PRIVATE ROAD. We found two stone cottages and a stone church surrounded by lilacs, vinca, tulips, marigolds, sun in and out, silence and solitude. No poplars anywhere, but Hopkins might have loved walking here.—L.S.

We returned to Balliol College and talked with Assistant Librarian Allen Tadiello. He directed us to GMH's rooms we'd seen last night, as well as a garret window overlooking another quad. In the quiet, Gothic library, he gave us an armful of GMH books—correspondence, journals, facsimiles of poems and notebooks, great stuff. Rather than being a loner, GMH knew plenty of other poets. The Hopkinses knew the Rosettis, who lived down the hill from them in Hampstead, and GMH may have even borrowed his style from Christina Rossetti. The jumble of connections is like a map of Wales, a veritable web. Christ Church meadows this morning was a large, loping place—I could imagine GMH walking there and breathing easily. Fretty chervil? and cow parsnip, cows and a path, a cottage being thatched, an open, uncut meadow.—M.S.

Edgbaston, England: Gates of The Oratory, a Roman Catholic church and boys' school built under the direction of Cardinal Newman.

At The Oratory, Hopkins was received into the Catholic church in 1866 by Cardinal Newman. A year later, Gerard Manley Hopkins taught classics there at the school.

Just went to Mass at The Oratory in Edgbaston, Birmingham. Yes! We found it easily, on Hagley Rd. It is a beautiful domed church, large, with a choir to rival King's College, Cambridge.

And our unknowing timing was right—after taking a few outside photos of it we went in, and the Catholic mass had just started.—L.S.

Roehampton, England: Southwest of the center of London is Manresa House, where Hopkins spent three tours: in 1868, he entered his novitiate, in 1873, he taught classics to Jesuit students, and in 1881 he began his tertianship.

The Catholic mass at The Oratory—High and Holy Mass, like going to Heaven without dying, great Romanesque arches, stars on ceiling. I can imagine why GMH wanted to become a Catholic. I had to restrain myself from doing the same. Exquisitely painful Gregorian chants, incense swung constantly during prayers. Chants in Latin.—M.S.

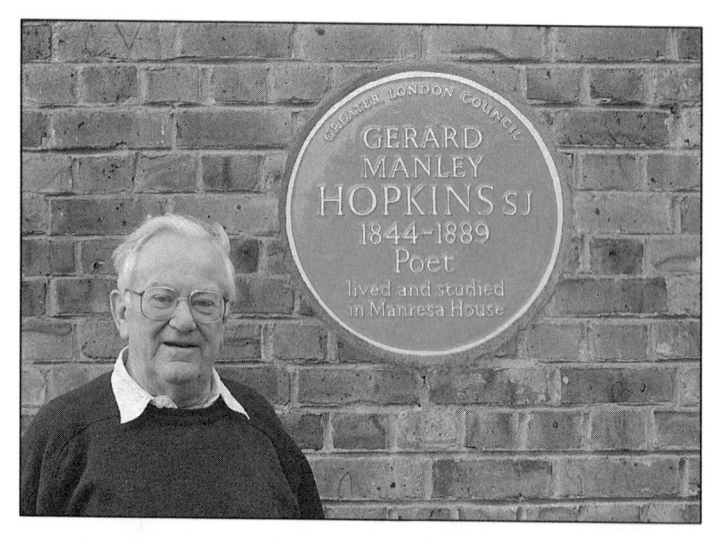

Michael Bampton, retired professor of Manresa House, Roehampton, showed us around the former Jesuit school.

A rough and adrenaline-pumping race around the perimeter of London, using narrow roundabouts. We arrived somehow where we wanted to be, Manresa House, where GMH spent four years in all. We were told to "ring up" Michael Bampton, historian of Hopkins-at-Manresa-House, who hurried over from his home and fortuitously provided us with our own tour. Jesuits, he told us, never walked down the center of the halls, for humility's sake. Sister Emmerich's garden agony account was read in what is now the Dining Hall. Hopkins "taught English badly" in a restored room upstairs. Descendants of the bluebells GMH drew in his journal are still rising.—M.S.

A kind Jesuit priest by the name of Paul Edwards lives at St. Beuno's and has written books and articles on Hopkins.

St. Asaph, Wales: In 1874, Hopkins began his study of theology at St. Beuno's College. Now a retreat center led by Jesuits, it is still out in the country, perched on a high hill overlooking the Vale of Clwyd.

Driving through Tremeirchion, Luci veered off to take a picture she'd just said she wanted: sheep on steep hillside with trees at top of hill. As we pulled over, we noticed over the door of an old house something in Welsh: "Ffynnon Beuno," meaning Beuno's Well. We'd been looking for St. Beuno's, where GMH went to school! I asked the owner of the house if St. Beeyuno's were around here. "St. Bino's," he said very kindly. "That's about 3/4 of a mile from here." We talked about "JER-rard" Hopkins for a while, then he gave us the same directions everyone else has been giving us: "It's just up the road; you can't miss it."—M.S.

St. Beuno's, high on a hill, almost hidden in trees. Overwhelming—slopes thick with bluebells, snowdrops, pale green-gold coins of new leaves. Photographed flowers, chestnut leaves, paths;

everything was written and illuminated in gold and magic and the sense that God had revealed all this to us.

Talked with Paul Edwards, a Hopkins scholar, as we wandered through the building. I photographed the row of rooms where he

From this pulpit in St. Beuno's dining hall, Hopkins gave "practice sermons."

lived—though he was then unrecognized, "just a bloke then," as a Jesuit brother told us. Edwards felt that though GMH was so sensitive to nature, he was not attuned to people and their level of understanding, one reason he was not a good teacher or a powerful preacher. Outside he showed us the terraced hillside, now gone wild, but bright with flowers in Hopkins' time. Marg sketched and I photographed leisurely. The day grey and unclear but the greens of leaves and lush undergrowth seemed to achieve a new intensity, almost stinging the eyes. We took a footpath over stiles and up the meadows behind Ffynnon Beuno. Saw a pheasant among the sheep. A cuckoo called clearly. The green was dotted for miles with sheep and cows, the air so still you could hear them grazing across the divide of air.—L.S.

I can understand why GMH wanted to live his whole life in the Vale of Clwyd and wrote almost half his poems here. Paul Edwards showed us all around St. Beuno's today. He showed us the dining room where GMH did his practice sermons at dinnertime, saying the others probably giggled, making neither heads nor tails of them. When I asked, "Why did he *practice* sermons?" he looked at me and asked, "Why does *anyone* practice *anything?*" He showed us the recreation room where after supper one night Hopkins might have been informally talking to the rector about the news of the wreck of the *Deutschland*. As we walked through St. Beuno's, I showed Father Edwards three of my poems: "Bleed beauty," "Bluebell," and "A sad and holy struggle." He read each one and gently handed them back, saying nothing, but I wasn't hurt by this. Like showing him a flower and him smiling yes. Somehow, I felt it was exactly what GMH would have done as a Jesuit at St. Beuno's.—M.S.

Went to Holywell, where we found, not surprisingly, a holy well, St. Winefred's, visited by Hopkins. He hiked there—nearly 30 miles! At "Pilgrim's Rest" Inn, we had a fine lunch served by a

Holywell, Wales: Old entrance to St. Winefred's Well, which Hopkins often visited during his time at St. Beuno's.

nun, Sister Margaret, who played Taizé music and Irish songs for our pleasure.—L.S.

GMH may well have stopped at the inn himself, because the Jesuits were connected with it in the 1870s. He was so enamored with the well that he began a play, "St. Winefred's Well," on the legend. I found some intriguing lines today from that play:

> Her eyes, oh and her eyes!
> In all her beauty, and sunlight
> to it is a pit, den, darkness,
> Foam-falling is not fresh to it. . . .

But the well water wasn't glacier blue anymore, as GMH had described it. It was a disappointing yellowish pool like the one you'd imagine at Bethesda. Just some giggly teenagers taking pictures down there, no pilgrims getting healed.—M.S.

Took the underground through London and walked to 111 Mount St., where Hopkins lived while preaching at the Farm St. Catholic Church nearby. More walking, more underground and a cab up to St. Charles Place where we found a Carmelite monastery but no chapel of Poor Clares—L.S.

The aging, slightly inebriated manager of the flats at 111 Mount St. was most congenial. After we'd rung the bell, he came up behind us on the stoop and asked, "Are you looking for me?"

—Hello, I'm Margaret Smith, and this—
—Are you, now?

—Yes. And this is Luci Shaw. We're doing a book project on the life of Gerard Hopkins, who was a poet in the 19th century and lived here in one of your flats for a while.

London: In 1878, Hopkins preached for only six months to the large, affluent congregation of Farm Street Church. It was apparently not his cup of tea.

—Well, that was before my time.
—Yes, he lived here in the 1870s or so.
—That *was* before my time.

Hopkins lived at 111 Mount Street, just behind Farm Street Church and separated by a little green.

—Yes, I believe you. We were trying to find out if we might be able to take a picture from upstairs, looking out.
—Well now, you'd have to ask one of the tenants to do that. All the flats are filled.
—Oh. Well, thanks very much. Sorry to bother you.
—(To Luci) Isn't she lovely? (To me) Are you married?
—Yes.
—Bloody fool.
—(Luci) I'm married, too.
—You're both bloody fools!
—Well, thanks for your help . . . goodbye!

On to what I had hoped would be the best and quietest and most *answering* place, at least of the day, perhaps of the trip: the chapel of Poor Clares. I thought if it were still there it might be just what I needed to find out why GMH had walked all the way from Hyde Park to pray there in 1867. It seems like such a strange thing for an Anglican man to do! I still don't understand. A woman at a Carmelite monastery kindly told us we would not see the chapel of Poor Clares, unfortunately, since they'd moved away to the country and the place has been made into a set of flats called Clare Gardens.—M.S.

"Clare Gardens"—a disappointment. Like the Hampstead flats they'd received an "architectural award," which seems to happen whenever a bit of GMH history is removed.—L.S.

Why are we not surprised to find Newman House, in process of renovation, open to the public only since yesterday? A young, enthusiastic woman led us up to the top story to GMH's actual room during his years in Dublin. It's the place more closely iden-

Dublin: Hopkins spent his last years feeling like an exile from England, teaching at University College, Dublin. From 1885-89, he lived here in Newman House.

Across the street from Newman House is St. Stephen's Green, where Hopkins must have walked many times.

tified with him personally than any we've seen thus far. Photographs: the room, Newman House, chestnut trees, and willows over pond in St. Stephen's Green.—L.S.

His room seemed like a lonely place, way up in the garret, all plain, except for some bad scrollwork on the ceiling. I think his sense of beauty must have been snubbed by this. I felt very close to him up there. I wished I could have stayed there with him for a while, when he was alive. I would have sat with him not talking. Then we would have discussed his terrible sonnets, and he may have felt released from some pressure—he would have been strengthened, I hope, by the scrap of redemption I'd brought him.—M.S.

Monasterevin, Ireland: On the road from Dublin to Galway is the small town of Monasterevin, which Hopkins liked to visit on holiday from University College. Here at Monasterevin House he often visited an elderly widow named Miss Cassidy.

Richard O'Rourke, the chemist at Monasterevin, took Marg and me under his kind wing and showed or told us everything he knew about GMH—showing us, by car, Moore Abbey, the "burling Barrow brown," a tree he thought GMH had sketched, the house where GMH visited Miss Cassidy (now the Presentation convent), the train station. He was so kind, endlessly kind, as have been so many in Ireland and Wales.—L.S.

Richard O'Rourke, local chemist and Vice-President of the International Hopkins Society, gave us an impromptu tour of the town.

While Luci was photographing, Richard O'Rourke told me in his low-key lilt that the idea for the Annual International Hopkins Summer School came a few years ago when a couple of them were sitting in the pub a few doors down from Monasterevin House during the town's July festival and agreed they should raise the level of the festival a bit by holding a poetry reading. They invited all the Irish poets and three declined, he said. I love the humor here.—M.S.

Early, in bright chilly sun, we visited the Glasnevin Cemetery where Hopkins is buried in the Jesuit community grave. We dropped three grass daisies on his engraved name, took its photo,

Dublin: We arrived in Dublin after crossing the Irish Sea by ferry, discovering that our Bed and Breakfast was within walking distance of Hopkins' gravesite in Glasnevin Cemetery.

and grieved awhile. The place is rich with intricately carved Celtic crosses and stone angels.—L.S.

PHOTO LOG

In Foreword:
Punting on the Thames, Oxford. A favorite pastime of GMH.

In Author's Preface:
Bluebells, Manresa House, Roehampton, England.
Inscape, St. Beuno's, St. Asaph, Wales.
Side door, St. Asaph Cathedral, St. Asaph.
Tudor house, Old Beaconsfield, England.
Willow, Christ Church meadows, Oxford.
Bluebells, St. Beuno's.

In Poetry Section, Opposite These Sonnets:
1. Christ Church meadows, Oxford.
2. Courtyard, The Oratory, Edgbaston, England.
4. Candles, St. Aloysius Roman Catholic Church, Oxford.
7. Woods behind St. Beuno's.
9. Chapel where GMH was ordained, St. Beuno's.
11. Ruins of Denbigh Castle, which GMH walked to from St. Beuno's, Denbigh, Wales.
12. Sheep in meadow, St. Asaph.

14. Cathedral spire, Coventry, England.
17. Cemetery monument, Old Beaconsfield, England.
19. Stone angels, Glasnevin Cemetery, Dublin.
21. Front garden, Ffynnon Beuno (Beuno's Well), Tremeirchion, Wales.
24. Attic bedroom-study of GMH, Newman House, University College, Dublin.
25. Interior, Monasterevin House, Monasterevin, Ireland.
27. Hillside, Vale of Clwyd, Wales.
29. Bluebells, St. Beuno's.
30. Tree-lined road in front of St. Beuno's.
32. Pigeons in Old Coventry Cathedral, Coventry.
33. Light on leaves, Tremeirchion, Wales.
35. Fenced countryside, Binsey, where GMH liked to walk from Oxford.
37. Tanglewood near Glendalough, Ireland.
39. Interior, St. Aloysius Roman Catholic Church, Oxford, where GMH worked as assistant pastor.
42. Firmly shut door, medieval convent, Coventry.
44. Path, St. Beuno's.

NOTES ON THE SONNETS

About his cycle of *Sonnets to Orpheus* Rainier Marie Rilke wrote to Countess Margot Sizzo-Noris-Crouy in 1923,

> These strange Sonnets were no intended or expected work; they appeared, often many in one day, completely unexpectedly. I could do nothing but surrender, purely and obediently, to the dictation of this inner impulse.

Not having heard of *Sonnets to Orpheus* (trans. Stephen Mitchell. New York: Touchstone, 1985) until after writing most of *A Holy Struggle,* I happened to run across Rilke's book in a New York bookstore. What Rilke described to the countess is what I experienced myself in the winter of 1990, especially for a few weeks in January and February when everyone but my husband was home with the flu. I would promise the boys some soup and company, "as soon as I finish one more sonnet!"

The date after each poem title tells when I wrote the first draft of that poem. Most of the writings quoted here and in the poem's epigraphs have been abbreviated. To relieve some confusion, the real Gerard Manley Hopkins is abbreviated GMH; the character Hopkins in my sonnets is simply H. In these notes I don't mean to decode all the allusions. I do want to give credit, though I will still be indebted, to Hopkins. Here are forty-four sonnets, for the number of years that he lived.

PART ONE

1. "Unkempt," Jan. 23, 1990. In his journal entry of May 2, 1866 GMH wrote:

Weather cold and raw. Swallows playing over Ch. Ch. (Christ Church, Oxford) meadows. Coaching with W.H. Pater this term. Case at one of the cricket grounds saw three Ch. Ch. men laughing loudly at a rat with back broken, a most ghastly sight, flying at a dog. He kicked away the dog, put his heel on the rat's head and killed it, and drove away the crowd of cads.

2. "Plain words enough," Jan. 22, 1990. The 1867 journal entry of GMH that nudged me to write this sonnet began, "To the chapel of poor clares, where I made my resolution, 'if it is better,' but now nothing is decided."

3. "For the novice at poor clares," Dec. 17, 1989. Early in the sonnet-making weeks, I began to draw ideas from Sonnet 34 of GMH that begins, "As kingfishers catch fire, dragonflies draw flame." Throughout my cycle you can find some reference to almost every line of this sonnet of his. For instance, dragonflies are mentioned twice in *A Holy Struggle;* "kingfisher" is used as an adjective, and the "catch fire/draw flame" metaphor appears with a twist.

"A halo rhymes the moon" comes from a journal musing of GMH dated Feb. 23, 1872: "A lunar halo: I looked at it from the upstairs library window. It fell in on the nether left hand side to rhyme the moon itself."

4. "This cave inside me," July 3, 1990. Months after writing "Unkempt" I wondered what had happened to the dead rat at Christ Church, Oxford. The rat becomes a symbol of some unnamed thing in H's life that at first is only offensive, but later, stale and loathsome. The play of light and dark shows up in poems of GMH like "The Lantern Out of Doors," and it shows up here in this sad poem.

5. "Which draws the world," Jan. 19, 1990. I asked myself what temptation there was in painting and not in music that put such a "strain upon the passions"! I thought the temptation might have been in the smell of oil paints, which my college art teacher directed us to enjoy. But in his letter to his friend Baillie GMH said it was "the higher and more attractive parts of the art," not the smell of paint, that strained the passions "which I think shd. be unsafe to encounter."

6. "Juice words," Jan. 23, 1990. The word "juice" is repeated throughout GMH's journal. It appears in his poems, too; he asks: "What is all this

juice and all this joy?" And he never misses a detail of the eye. In 1866 he scribbled down images concerning juices and eyes:

> Cups of the eyes, Gathering back the lightly hinged eyelids. Bows of the eyelids. Pencil of eyelashes. Juices of the eyeball. Eyelids like leaves, petals, caps, tufted hats. Juices of the sunrise.

7. "In certain light," Jan. 24, 1990. In an early diary entry in 1866, two years before he decided to become a Jesuit, GMH wrote out a few stringent guidelines for himself:

> For Lent. No puddings on Sundays. No tea except if to keep me awake and then without sugar. Meat only once a day. Not to sit in armchair except can work in no other way. Ash Wednesday and Good Friday bread and water.

For days I walked around with these guidelines circling in my head, along with a line that went, "I am afraid of too much _____." I wondered what it was that H feared most. Then I heard our pastor say, "We fear the world too much."

8. "Slaughter of the innocents," Dec. 12, 1989. This was the first sonnet I wrote from the viewpoint of H. It was December, and I was practicing with our choir the old Advent song concerning the Slaughter of the Innocents:

> Herod the king in his raging
> Charg-ed he hath this day
> His men of might in his own sight
> All children young to slay.

9. "Pity's not an image," Jan. 16, 1990. I wrote what I thought went through the mind of GMH as he wrote the single line in his early journal: "Moonlight hanging or dropping on trees like blue cobweb." Elizabeth Bishop helped here, with a stanza in her villanelle, "One Art":

> Even losing you (the joking voice, a gesture
> I love) I shan't have lied. It's evident
> the art of losing's not too hard to master

though it may look like (*Write* it!) like disaster.
(*The Complete Poems, 1927-1979.* New York: Farrar, Straus, & Giroux, 1983)

10. "Leaping under stress," April 10, 1990. In a letter to Bridges in 1881, GMH wrote, "One night, as I lay awake in a fevered state, I had some glowing thoughts and lines, but I did not put them down and I fear they may fade to little or nothing."

11. "Kidnappers," Jan. 31, 1990. The last entry in the extant journal of GMH is dated Feb. 7, 1875 (the year of the rebirth of his poetry). It reads:

> I asked Miss Jones the Welsh word for fairy, for we were translating Cinderella. She told me cipenaper: the word is nothing but kidnapper, from cipio, to snatch away. She told me quite simply that she had seen the fairies on the Holywell road. She was going up at five o'clock in the morning, when she saw three little boys wearing little frock coats and odd little caps running and dancing before her. She went on to the house and wondered that children could be out so early. "Why, she has seen the kidnappers" her grandmother said.

12. "Not willing to go," Dec. 28, 1989. Though he rarely mentioned the "slaughter," GMH must have mourned the poems he burned.

13. "The air like wine," Jan. 24, 1990. On Aug. 30, 1867, GMH wrote in his journal, "Fair; in afternoon fine; the clouds had a good deal of crisping and mottling."

A few days before writing this poem I read in *The New York Times Book Review* a reference to a short story by Raymond Carver. The reviewer wrote that the rolls offered by a baker to a grieving couple in the story was " 'a small, good thing,' a taste of redemption." It occurred to me that this was just what H needed from the novice from Poor Clares.

PART TWO

14. "A jar of tulips," Jan. 25, 1990. In his journal GMH wrote in July, 1868:

Started with Ed. Bond for Switzerland. But Basel at night! A woman came to a window with a candle and some mess she was making, and then that was gone and there was no light anywhere but the moon.

GMH must have created his own poem, "The Candle Indoors," from this journal entry. Edward was not a Jesuit brother, as I imply in the sonnets, but a friend from Oxford. A few days after writing this entry GMH wrote about a Swiss guide who told him: "Le bon Dieu n'est pas comme ca" ("The good Lord is not like that"). I think the conversation must have had to do with penance.

15. "One ventures further in," Jan. 26, 1990. On the same trip to Switzerland, GMH wrote a metaphor for nearly every rock and fall he and Edward encountered while hiking. I like the July 20 entry, describing a glacier's ice cave:

We went into the grotto. It looked like a blue tent and as you went further in changed to lilac. As you come out the daylight glazes the groins with gleaming rosecolour.

16. "Not the place," April 9, 1990. Still in Switzerland, on July 25 GMH wrote:

Up at two to ascend the Breithorn. Stars twiring (sic) brilliantly. Taurus up, a pale light stressily edging the eastern skyline. Mountain summits are not the places for mountain views. Then the cold feet, the spectacles, the talk and the lunching came in. Even with one companion ecstasy is almost banished.

17. "Agony," Feb. 3, 1990. In Roehampton, London in Feb. 1870 GMH wrote this entry:

They were reading Sister Emmerich's account of the Agony in the Garden and I suddenly began to cry and sob and could not stop. I stood wondering at myself not seeing in my reason the traces for an adequate cause for such strong emotion—the traces I say because of course the causes in itself is adequate for the sorrow of a lifetime. A sharp knife does not cut for being pressed as long as it is pressed without any shaking of the hand. But one touch may be so delicate that the pathos seems to have gone directly to the body and cleared the understanding in its passage.

The words were all there. Very little rewriting was needed to make this journal entry into a sonnet. I did add one thought at the end that H might think to himself but never say aloud.

18. "Prometheus," Jan. 26, 1990. "Haggard," I found, literally means *wild hawk*. See Donne's sonnet 14, "Batter my heart, three-personed God," for "b" words, such as *break, blow, burn*. See also Hopkins' sonnet:

> O the mind, mind has mountains; cliffs of fall
> Frightful, sheer, no-man-fathomed. Hold them cheap
> May who ne'er hung there.

After writing "Prometheus" I saw that Hopkins mentioned the contemporary play Prometheus in a letter to Bridges, commenting drily that the story was "scarcely meant for acting."

19. "Turning the earth," Sept. 27, 1990. I wrote this one after pulling weeds in front of our chapel steps.

20. "Raisin cakes," Jan. 26, 1990. In 1872 GMH wrote in his journal that on holiday on the Isle of Man he had first begun to get hold of *Sentences* by Duns Scotus. "And just when I took in any inscape of the sky or sea," he said, "I thought of Scotus."

21. "Settled for the black cloth," Jan. 27, 1990. "From Hodder Wood we walked on the other side of the river," GMH wrote in his journal in 1873. I thought "we" might mean Edward and wondered what Edward would say about the novice from Poor Clares. Edward seems to be a practical man, faithful without thinking about it, funny without meaning to be. Not a poet himself, Edward speaks here in blank verse.

22. "The lady's eyes," Jan. 22, 1990. A ripe acorn dropping to the ground without producing offspring seemed the right image for a celibate man like GMH.

In some poems GMH writes about the violence of attraction to "mortal beauty." But always he adds that giving beauty "back to God, beauty's self and beauty's giver" is the chief end of that matter.

23. "Blue behind the veil," Jan. 29, 1990. At the Isle of Man on Aug. 10, 1872 GMH wrote in his journal about the high waves and the rocks, "The breakers are rolled out just as a piece of putty between the palms. It is pretty to see the dance and swagging of the light green tongues of waves in a place locked between rocks."

24. "The sea rain," May 4, 1990. On Aug. 4, 1873, after another vacation at Isle of Man, GMH wrote this entry:

> At eight we sailed for Liverpool in wind and rain. I think it is the salt that makes the rain at sea sting so much. There was a good-looking young man on board who got drunk and sang, "I want to go home to Mamma." From Blackburn I walked: infinite stiles and sloppy fields. We went to the College, almost no gas, therefore candles in bottles, things not ready, darkness and despair.

25. "The mystery of Grace," Nov. 27, 1990. There is a wonderful part in a Platonic dialogue that GMH wrote, concerning two Oxford men:

> "But" went on the Professor "if I am to undertake the analysis of so subtle a piece of beauty as you have tasked me with, might I do it by the aid of candlelight? for it is now dark, you see, and wet underfoot and one is almost cold, I think. I hope the tea is not."
> "Ah! the tea" said Hanbury; and they went in.

26. "A lost one," April 14, 1990. This sonnet was taken from two entries of GMH. One entry, dated Sept. 24, 1870, is a long, colorful description of the Northern Lights. The other, from Spring 1872, is a short complaint about the felling of an ash grove nearby, for which he wrote his own poem. I switched the order of these entries and placed them close to one another to show a gradual reopening of H's heart.

27. "Bleed beauty," Jan. 29, 1990. About GMH's inspiration for "The Wreck of *The Deutschland,*" Peter Milward writes in his book *Landscape and Inscape:*

What he put at the centre of his poem was not so much the wreck of *The Deutschland* nor the fate of the five nuns, but the call of the tall nun, "O Christ, Christ, come quickly!" It was evidently this cry of hers, uttered from her heart, that appealed to the heart of the poet.

28. "Seven years," Jan. 30, 1990. GMH ends his poem, "To What Serves Mortal Beauty?" with these lines:

> What do, then? how meet beauty? Merely meet it; own,
> Home at heart, heaven's sweet gift; then leave, let that alone.
> Yea, wish that though, wish all, God's better beauty, grace.

PART THREE

29. "Bluebell," Feb. 2, 1990. This is a left-hand-rhyme sonnet. In a journal entry dated May 9, 1871 GMH wrote:

> The bluebells in your hand baffle you with their inscape, made to every sense: the long stalks make a brittle rub and jostle like the noise of a hurdle strained against; then there is the faint honey smell and in the mouth the sweet gum when you bite them. But this is easy, it is the eye they baffle. They give one a fancy of panpipes and a wind instrument with stops.

30. "This pure world," July 24, 1990. I read an ancient waka written by the woman poet Izumi Shikibu and translated by Jane Hirschfield:

> One by one,
> at day's end,
> the birds take flight
> in all directions—
> which could lead me to you?
> *(The Ink Dark Moon.* New York: Charles Scribners, 1988)

The end couplet of "This pure world" has six beats per line, a lengthening that writers of sonnets have used sometimes for effect.

31. "At zenith," March 14, 1990. This begins a dream sequence, which ends at "Fugue." GMH was intrigued with points on natural objects like

stars, horns and leaves. He made up words like *quains* and *margaretting* to describe this outwaving. About clouds he wrote, "Possibly each tuft is quained and a crystal."

32. "A wet flaming," Feb. 1, 1990. GMH wrote in his journal entry of June 16, 1873:

> I looked at the pigeons down in the kitchen yard. Their pins are like cuttleshells found on the shore. The others are dull thundercolour. As one moved its head a crush of satin green came and went, a wet or soft flaming of light. Sometimes I hear the cuckoo with clear and fluty notes: it is when the hollow of a rising ground conceives them and palms them up.

And to his sister Kate he wrote on April 25, 1871 about lambs, "Our fields are full of them. When they were a little younger and nicer and sillier they would come gamboling up as if one were their mother. One of them sucked my finger and my companion took another up in his arms."

33. "Clair-obscure," Feb. 2, 1990. A month after writing the entry about the pigeons GMH wrote, "Very hot, though the wind dappled very sweetly on one's face and when I came out I seemed to put it on like a gown as a man puts on the shadow he walks into." See GMH's poem, "Spring and Fall," which begins,

> Margaret, are you grieving
> Over Goldengrove unleaving?

34. "Holy company," March 30, 1990. The fishing images come from our two years in a fishing village in Southeast Alaska.

35. "Languishing," Feb. 5, 1990. There seems to be no way to overstate the passionate intensity of the real GMH, no way to exaggerate the discipline he placed on that intensity. For GMH the harshest regimen might have been the practice the Jesuits called "discipline of the eyes." For at least one six-month period he did not allow himself to look up from the ground.

In his introduction to the Penguin edition of GMH's writings, W.H. Gardner describes St. Ignatius Loyola, the ascetic founder of the Society of Jesus, as a formative influence. "The full force of the impact upon Hopkins of the Ignatian discipline," Gardner says, "with its supreme ideal of Sacrifice," is brought out in many of his poems.

(Poems and Prose of Gerard Manley Hopkins: Selected with an Introduction and Notes by W.H. Gardner. Baltimore, Md.: Penguin Books, 1963)

36. "No relief," Feb. 5, 1990. To symbolize the frustration of GMH in his later years over not "breeding one work that wakes," I wrote this fragment of a sonnet. The night before, I had heard a local news report about a ship docked in New York Harbor that was listing badly. Rescue teams tried adding ballast and a number of other tricks, but when the tide came in the ship righted itself.

37. "Fugue," Jan. 30, 1990. A unfinished poem by GMH, titled "Epithalamion," which was scrawled on the back of an examination paper while he was professor of classics in Dublin, begins:

> Make believe
> We are leafwhelmed somewhere with the hood
> Of some branchy bunchy bushybowered wood,
> Southern dene or Lancashire clough or Devon cleave,
> That leans along the loins of hills.

I had known only one definition of "fugue," a musical term. But after writing the sonnet I found in *The American Heritage Dictionary* a second definition. Literally, "flight," a fugue is a time of amnesia "during which the patient is apparently conscious of his actions but on return to normal has no recollection of them."

38. "Revelation," March 14, 1990. For this and the previous sonnet I thought of the first chapter in Song of Solomon, where the Lover says, "Behold, you are beautiful, my beloved, truly lovely. Our couch is green; the beams of our house are cedar."

39. "Beside me empty," Feb. 1, 1990. GMH wrote a letter to Baillie on May 22, 1880, saying,

At least I can say my Liverpool work is very harassing and makes it hard to write. Tonight I am sitting in my confessional, but the faithful are fewer than usual and I am unexpectedly delivered from a sermon which otherwise I should have had to be delivered of. Here comes someone.

In "Beside me empty," I picked up the story where it left off. H finds that the "someone" is Grace. He blesses her with a benediction, an unknowing goodbye.

40. "A lovely creature," May 10, 1990. A starling did cruise through our chapel a few months earlier, making a spectacle of itself. I had written a scattered poem about it at the time but put it away, unfinished. In May I realized that H might find a reason and a name for the stranger.

41. "In orchards not kept," June 2, 1991. The final poem I added to this collection had its beginnings two years before in Wisconsin. There a ripe apple did drop into my hand. I wrote out the sonnet without GMH in mind, never thinking of including it in *A Holy Struggle* until Luci suggested it.

42. "Cloistered," Feb. 5, 1990. The idea for the story in this sonnet comes straight from a scene in "The Sound of Music."

43. "Keep Grace," Feb. 3, 1990. While waiting at the doctor's office I scribbled this on the back of a copy of "Beside me empty." I thought to finish it later but decided against it.

44. "A sad and holy struggle," Feb. 5, 1990. In my own journal the previous fall I wrote down the seeds for this sonnet.

BIBLIOGRAPHY

Edwards, Paul, *Canute's Tower, St. Beuno's,* Fowler Wright Books, Leominster, 1990.

Hopkins, Gerard Manley, *The Early Poetic Manuscripts and Notebooks of Gerard Manley Hopkins in Facsimile,* Norman MacKenzie, ed., Garland Publishing, London, 1989.

——, *Gerard Manley Hopkins: A Selection of his Poems and Prose,* W.H. Gardner, ed., The Penguin Poets, London, 1960.

——, *Gerard Manley Hopkins: Selected Letters,* Catherine Phillips, ed., Clarendon Press, Oxford, 1990.

——, *The Poems of Gerard Manley Hopkins,* W.H. Gardner and N.H. MacKenzie, ed., Oxford University Press: Oxford, 1990.

Martin, Robert Bernard, *Gerard Manley Hopkins: A Very Private Life,* HarperCollins, London, 1991.

Milward, Peter, *Landscape and Inscape: Vision and Inspiration in Hopkins's Poetry,* Wm. B. Eerdmans, Grand Rapids, 1975.

Renascence, "Gerard Manley Hopkins, 1889-1989," Vol. XLII, Nos. 1-2, Marquette University Press, Milwaukee, Fall 1989-Winter 1990.

Ruggles, Eleanor, *Gerard Manley Hopkins: A Life,* W.W. Norton & Company, New York, 1944.

Watson, J.R., *The Poetry of Gerard Manley Hopkins,* Penguin Books, London, 1989.

The Way Supplement, "Spirituality and the Artist: Essays in Honour of Gerard Manley Hopkins, 1844-1889," Number 66, The Way Publications, London, Autumn 1989.